Free Stuff
Everyday

Free Stuff Everyday

Mike Essex

Lotus Publishing
Chichester, England

First published in 2011 by

Lotus Publishing, Apple Tree Cottage, Inlands Road, Nutbourne, PO18 8RJ

Text Design Wendy Craig
Cover Design Jim Wilkie
Printed and Bound in the UK by Bell and Bain

British Library Cataloguing-in-Publication Data
A CIP record for this book is available from the British Library
ISBN 978 1 905367 34 4

About the Author

When not teaching people how to get free stuff, Mike works at a digital marketing agency. He lives in Southampton with his wife Marie, three cats and an evil (but lovable) dog.

This book is for my wife Marie and my parents,
who prove the best things in life are free

chapter 1

One Core Principle

It doesn't matter who you are, your job title, personal status or age – there is a company out there who will want you to have their product for free.

Once you understand this principle, it becomes far easier to move away from using vouchers, and to move towards contacting companies directly. In addition, it will help you feel empowered that by following the steps in this book you will get freebies.

This is more than just the power of positive thinking, or a delusional message to trick you into reading more. It's a simple fact, based on my own experience and the mindset of companies large and small.

Whether you exude confidence or are shy as a mouse, there is a method you can use, and this book will arm you with all the information you need.

Fancy a Free Lunch?

To prove this point, let's assess the age old saying, "There's no such thing as a free lunch." On face value, this statement is wrong. After all, you could get lunch without spending any money thanks to a generous friend, a giveaway of product samples or a work conference with catering.

Peel back the veil a little further and we see that each of these "free" offerings comes with a prospective price tag. Your generous friend may expect you to return the favour one day. The product sample giveaway is on the hope you'll one day buy the product, and the work conference comes with you having to listen to the associated presentation or meeting. Even something that may seem a selfless act – such as food at a wedding – is there to get you to attend. There is always a cost, even if not financial.

Companies are the same – they will be more than happy to give you something on the basis that they can get something in return. Typically this is money, but there are lots of other things you can offer companies that are worth far more than money.

What's In It for Companies?

In fact, there are lots of things you can offer companies that require very little work on your part – such as reviews, product feedback and brand loyalty. By offering something to a company in return for their product, you are creating a link that not only encourages them to provide you with one free product, but with many products over time.

Companies have been giving their products away for years. You only have to browse a voucher website or walk around a shopping centre to see that free samples are big business, and that companies will do anything to encourage customers to try their product.

In these days of 24/7 communications we're less receptive to advertising than ever and sometimes the only way a company can get people to try their product is to thrust a free sample in their face. Even then, they'll often find their product left at the bottom of a bag, or passed around friends and family until someone throws it away.

We can use this desire they have for you to try their product to our advantage. Let's imagine I have been a fan of a particular brand of Cheddar for years but am becoming a bit bored with it. So I write to different companies that sell cheese explaining that I'd like to try something new.

Those companies who respond are in effect trying to buy my loyalty with their free samples. All I am offering in return is the potential that I may like their brand enough to buy more in the future. No guarantees, no lies or trickery, just a simple request.

For the company this is a massive opportunity to get me hooked on their product and to lure me away from a competitor, which is a far sweeter victory. The effort on my part is minor, and yet I've created a need that companies will want to fulfil.

I could expand this further by holding a cheese-tasting club with friends, or promising to score each cheese out of ten and write about them online. This would create an even larger need, and make companies more likely to send me free products. The snowball effect once you find a winning formula like the one above is massive, and yet it is born out of a single core principle. It can also fit around your life. In this example, I can send a few letters after my day job and try the cheeses at my own pace.

What's In It for Me?

Contacting companies in this way is infinitely more valuable to you too than simply browsing shopping centres and websites looking for deals of the day. Rather than one-off samples (that more often than not are all gone before you even see them), you are asking for full versions of products.

You are creating a need for companies to fill and establishing yourself as an opportunity for their brand. In doing so, you will rise above the millions of people looking for a pointless freebie, and create a persona that really speaks to the company.

There are a few steps in this process – such as deciding what you want for free, and how you will get it – but that's what this book explains in more detail. I've tried to provide a solution for everyone, whether you love talking or are shy. If you really love the web there are some fantastic ways to define yourself as an ambassador for free things online; and if you want to do something as simple as starting a book club with friends offline, that's covered too.

The ideas you use for convincing a company to send you something for free will all hark back to this core principle, and it's vital you remember that asking a company for a free product is no different than them putting an advert in your favourite magazine. They want to reach customers who understand their brands. You want to reach companies and understand their products. The link between your needs and the needs of the company are the same – so let's work on getting you both connected.

What If Everyone Does It?

So this would be a pretty flawed system if it couldn't scale to some extent. After all, there'd be no point me telling you all these tips if I also couldn't also use them on a day-to-day basis. In fact, the more people that use these tips, the better it will be for everyone.

Let's say I contact a company that has never given something away before. Through the ideas in this book I'm able to convince them to part with a product, and they're impressed by what they receive in return. When you then contact this company they'll already be receptive to giving products away, and it'll be far easier for you to negotiate a freebie as well.

The other way of looking at this is as a competition. Later I'll talk about creating an offer that encourages people to send you products, and this will help you to stand out from the crowd. This book is about creating ideas that make you attractive to companies – and because it isn't a "one-size-fits-all" solution, it means not everyone will be hitting every company with the exact same strategy.

I want to encourage people to try and stand out, and to appeal to companies in their own ways. I've included a ton of examples from my own experience, but you can take these ideas and develop them into something else. While I'll give you the tools, you can dig wherever you want. That's one of the reasons why this book works regardless of how many people act on it.

chapter 2

Bring Back Bartering

In the days before money everything was "free", or at least didn't have a financial cost associated with it. Instead people would "barter", offering one good or service in return for another. Sometimes the ratio wouldn't be exact, so multiple products would be used to purchase a single service. I vote we bring this back!

Even when money was introduced, bartering remained an effective way of surviving when times were tight, or when you simply couldn't find someone else who had money to purchase your product. For painters, this meant they would give paintings away in return for food and shelter. If you had a farm you'd swap produce for clothes, and generally the economy was founded on more than just numbers in a bank balance.

Despite still having abilities that others value, we tend mostly to accept money for the work we do. This is a shame, as it means the old principles of bartering have been lost, and this once-noble tradition has been replaced with corporate greed.

Bartering In the Modern Age

So I suggest we bring back bartering, especially as it will help no end with the goals we are trying to achieve. If companies want to give us stuff for free, then why not barter ourselves and our skills in return?

Want someone to mow your lawn for free? Well, why not do their taxes, wash their windows or write them a poem? Find out what they want in return and offer it to them. You'll get something without spending any money, and so will they. Both of you will benefit, and the good karma of bartering is more likely to make both of you do the same in the future.

Free things don't always have to come from companies that have multinational offices and thousands of staff (although I will certainly cover how to get free stuff from them too). Any local tradesman or small business should be used to the concept of bartering, especially if you have something they want in return.

If companies want you to have something for free, then it makes sense that you should want them to have something for free in return. Sure, it may seem that for something to be "free" it shouldn't require any effort on your part, but as with the free-lunch example we know that isn't always the case (and if it is, it'll be a one-off that won't be easy to repeat).

How Do Celebrities Do It?

Even those people in the public eye who are given things for free all the time are given them on the basis of "implied bartering". This is when someone gives a product away for free, on the assumption they will receive something in return.

A famous celebrity who is given a designer watch for free may not give something back in return. However, when the watch is given to them there is "implied bartering" as the company doing the giving assumes one of the following will occur:

1) *The celebrity will wear the watch in public*; this could cause it to be photographed and shown in a glossy magazine. People will then see it and try to copy the style by purchasing the watch.

2) *The watch will not be accepted*; in which case the bartering contract is refused and the company can try again with another celebrity.

3) *It opens a dialogue with the celebrity*; perhaps the watchmaker wants the celebrity to be their spokesperson? Giving them the product for free lets them test it and opens the door for future conversation.

4) *Future purchasing*; no celebrity lives on free stuff alone, so eventually they'll need to buy another watch. This could be another one from the same company that was nice enough to give them one for free.

These are just four possibilities in a much larger pool of outcomes, none of which the company can guarantee, but many of which result in extra exposure for their brand.

The celebrity can accept the watch and choose to do nothing, which is why the "implied" tag is added to the bartering process, but this is the risk the company makes giving something away without a guaranteed return.

It's the same risk as someone giving you a free product on the street. You may choose to use it, give it back, talk to the person giving it you, or buy more in the future. Even if you're not a celebrity, you're in the exact same position of power, under the same bartering rules.

The celebrity example is based on a company contacting them, but you can flip this around and contact a company, offering to do something in return for a free product. We could also use "implied bartering", by giving something to the company on the assumption that they could give something back.

How Can I Do It?

Let's say we start up a book club with some of our friends. We choose our book of the month from "Company X", buy the book and discuss it. We decide that we like the book and want to ask Company X to provide the next book for us to read.

At this point we have started the "informal bartering" procedure, as we have already purchased one of their books and are asking for something for free in return for exposing their books. Company X can therefore choose to send us a book, on the basis that the other book club members may buy more of their books in the future, or decline our request, in which case we can contact a different company. We may also decide to buy a Company X book anyway, depending on preferences.

Alternatively if we wanted to barter for real, making it "formal" bartering, we wouldn't buy a single Company X book and would only choose to talk about books in our book club that had been sent for free. We would call book companies offering to discuss their books, in return for being sent them.

This is another low-time-intensive strategy that has good potential for return, and through "formal" bartering we aren't spending any money and have much lower risk than with "informal" bartering. Our chance of success is slightly lower because we haven't shown any interest in Company X and their books, as we did in the "informal" example, so it's worth weighing up both options.

chapter 3

The Benefits for Brands

Although this book is written from a consumer perspective, every concept and solution can be turned around to create a great new way for a company to gain extra product exposure. The sort of customers who read this book and then contact brands asking for free stuff are 100% the ideal people to turn into brand advocates.

Where else will you find people who have actively sought out your brand, and who are prepared to offer something in return? Here's just a few of the ways you can use free stuff to gain increased sales and brand awareness (oh, and for customers reading this, here are some good ideas on things you can offer companies).

Market Research

Forget internal guesswork and mass surveys. The best way to gather effective research on what the market wants is to bring together your prospective customers and ask them. In return you can offer your product to them when it's completed, and it's also a nice way of showing them you listened to their ideas. They get free stuff, and you get actionable data.

Product Feedback

Similarly to market research, you can give people early versions of your products and ask them for their help and feedback. For the customer it's a great way to make them feel a part of something important and to reward any previous brand loyalty they may have had. For a brand, it's another way to build real customer data into your product development process.

Reviews and Testimonials

When your product has been released, reviews and testimonials are a great way to build some exposure for the product. It's recommended that brands start giving away products to reviewers 10 weeks before the official launch, as this can help generate an early buzz and it gives people a chance to fit the reviews in around their existing schedules.

To find people to review your product, search online for bloggers in your niche, or other active people in the print press or online environments. Then check if they've covered anything similar and make contact with them to see if they'd be interested. Don't send something to every person; those with the strongest websites and communities are your top priority.

Social Media Awareness

Competitions with free stuff tend to go viral very quickly on social media like Twitter and Facebook, especially if you are giving away something that people can't buy in a shop.

To capitalise on this, try to find something unique you can give away (e.g. your product in a different colour or packaging or with engravings, etc.) and mention this as a competition to people online. Make it so they have to display a message on their social profile in order to enter, and then other people in their network will do the same. It's a quick way to spread a message to a lot of people online, just by giving away one free thing.

Improving Local Awareness

If you want to raise awareness of your product in the local community, then giving a product away to vocal people in that community is a great start. Find local journalists or businesses and give them products to talk about.

Alternatively, pick random members of the public and give them something for free. You can be sure they'll tell their friends about it and help spread the word in the community. In addition, the unexpected nature ("Who will Company X pick next?") helps generate a talking point and a buzz about your product.

Building Loyal Customers

If your product is the first in a sequence (e.g. the first book in a trilogy), something people use often (e.g. cheese), or one that has future bolt-on purchases (e.g. a razor that needs replacement blades), then giving them away can encourage customers to make future purchases. People love free stuff, and the initial gesture can go a lot further than 50% discounts in getting people to reuse your brand in the future.

Proving Yourself

Regardless of whether you feel your product is the best, a customer would much rather be shown this fact than told it. If you can create a trial version of your product that can be given away for free, then it's a definite must for every business. Give people access to your product and prove to them that it is worth using on a regular basis. Alternatively, offer a 30-day trial or money-back guarantee to effectively give something away with the promise of extra income.

Building Business Connections

It's not just customers who like getting things for free – businesses do too. Whether it be a trial of your product, or a goodwill gesture, a free product is a nice way of building links with other businesses. For example, if you feel you'll need the services of a business in the future, then a free product now can work wonders in giving you an opportunity to speak to the right people later.

Generating Online Buzz

The Internet has generated millions of new places to get product exposure, and endless conversations that would be ideal places for your brand to be mentioned. Free products can lead to reviews, and they can also lead to links back to your website. From a search engine optimisation perspective, this is an excellent indicator to the search engines that your brand is being talked about and should therefore be displayed higher in search results – a great added bonus!

Improved Brand Perception

When choosing a brand, would a customer rather pick one they have never heard of, or one which they've heard about in competitions, or from people who got a freebie? It's a no-brainer, and an active brand, which isn't afraid to engage customers in multiple ways, is far more appealing.

Improved Customer Confidence

Only a brand that is confident in their product will be prepared to give it away. After all, people may write bad reviews, or be turned away from buying it in the future. However, by giving free stuff away you are allowing people to try before they buy, or giving people the chance to write good reviews. When other customers see these conversations, it gives them the confidence they need to trust your product in the future.

This is a small sampling of ideas, and there are plenty more ways to engage with customers throughout the book. By showing both sides of the argument, customers get more of a view of why these strategies work, and businesses get to see more of the benefits of why they should give stuff away. Free stuff for everyone!

chapter 4

The Rules

Before we get started, here are some quick ground rules:

1. Don't try to con a company or scam anyone.
2. Do not engage in any unlawful practices. Obey local laws at all times.
3. Do not blackmail a company or pressure them unnecessarily.
4. Be nice and don't engage in negative comments or insult companies.
5. Be safe. If a free product looks poorly made or dangerous, send it back.
6. Only accept free products from legitimate companies.
7. Watch out for online scams. Check companies online first.
8. Always state you will not return a free product when making contact.
9. Don't give away unnecessary personal details (passwords, card details, etc.).
10. Follow any other contracts you may have (e.g. your day job).
11. Don't lie when contacting companies or when covering their products.
12. If you offer something in return for a freebie, always ensure you do it.

chapter 5

Decide What You Want for Free

Easy, you say? What if I told you this is actually one of the hardest steps in the process?

It's not necessarily that many products are off limits or that there are lots of products it's impossible to get. I honestly believe you can get just about anything for free with the right research and offer – but it's still important to decide on the products you'd like for free and the extent you are willing to go to get them.

Another factor to consider is whether you want to focus on a category (e.g. any video camera), a brand (e.g. Sony) or a specific product (e.g. an X123 Megabrand Camera). Each of these types carries with it different experiences and will factor in to your success rate.

Target a Category

So if you've decided you want any video camera, you'll find quite a large number of companies who make that particular product. You can then target them all with the exact same pitch, because the product is exactly the same.

This is the quickest and easiest way to get something for free, and gives you lots of potential for success.

The downside is that once you have a free video camera, you may not want to focus on getting other video cameras, and will therefore need a new offer when you barter with other companies.

Target a Brand

Option two is to target a specific brand. This is an interesting solution as it means you can tailor your offer when you make contact and keep trying different methods until you find something the company wants in return for the free product.

You can then try other products the company makes, above and beyond your original free product, and build a long relationship with the company.

A negative factor is that you may be targeting a company that is simply unresponsive or only deals with members of the press. If this occurs, no matter how good your offer, it simply won't be possible to get something for free if they are unwilling to listen to what you have to say. Therefore this isn't a very effective long-term strategy.

Target a Product

The third option is to choose a very specific product type. This means you'll be focused very specifically on getting the product you want from the exact manufacturer. Although not impossible, this is the highest-risk option.

Not only do you have to convince the company to speak to you, but also to accept your offer and send you the product you want.

So if you pick a specific target then the number of products you could receive reduces as per the diagram below:

All of the above strategies are possible and I've used them with success in different guises, but if this is your first time I'd suggest you take the category approach. If a company is rude, you can simply move on to the next one with minimum fuss. You can create a single offer and apply it to multiple places – and once you see success, refine this offer for different categories of product in the future.

Decision Time

So let's first decide which category you want to go for. It's best to start with products over services, as these are far easier to get as freebies. And with services it's harder to guarantee they will continue to be free (e.g. you might be given your gas bill free for a year, then get stuck with the company for future years at a high price).

In terms of finding products, you may already have something in mind, or be pretty sure what you'd like. If that's the case then fantastic, but if not, don't worry. There are many different ways to identify which products you can get.

Pick up a catalogue and flick through the pages, search the Internet for new products or simply ask your friends if there's anything they'd like. I've even walked around town centres with a notepad writing down the types of products I'd like to get for free.

Finding Manufacturers

When you've got something in mind, the next stage in the process is to find as many manufacturers of that product as you can. We'll need to log all this information for future tracking, so open a spreadsheet and add the following columns:

- Product Type
- Manufacturer
- Product Name
- Website
- Score
- Comments

You'll be able to fill in the first four options by searching online for your category. In the video cameras example, if I enter the product into a search engine such as Google, I'm presented with all the manufacturers and can take their details one by one. Alternatively, if you've spotted the brands in a town centre you can search for their brand name online and make a note of the website.

For the product name column, add the product you'd like from that company. If you don't have a specific preference, that's fine too – just leave the column blank.

With the score column you're attempting to add a value out of ten based on how much you'd like that company's product. While I'm sure you'd like all of the brands for free, there will most likely be one that trumps the others, based on your own experiences with the brands, customer reviews or general opinion.

Adding these scores means you can better focus your efforts and ensure that the time you spend attempting to get freebies is proportionate to the returns. Those with higher scores get more of your time and are your first contacts, while those with lower scores become backups to approach if the others fail.

In the comments column you should add any information you see about the product that might help when you approach the company. This will be difficult for the first time, so look for the following:

- Have they launched a new product?
- Do they have reviews on other websites?
- Do they still make the product?
- Is their website updated often?

Knowing these factors will give you a clue as to how responsive the company will be, and whether the product is likely to be available for free.

Next we need to decide whom to contact...

chapter 6

Decide Whom to Contact

Once you've decided exactly what it is you'd like for free, it's key that you identify the best person to contact within that company. Once again the Internet is the best source of research in this area, as contact details are often posted online for companies big and small.

Before we start searching, we need to add the following new columns to our spreadsheet next to the company details:

- Contact Name
- Department (e.g. Marketing/Sales)
- Email Address
- Phone Number
- Postal Address
- Comments

That's a lot of prospective information, although you won't need every piece for every company. Grab the information you can, ensuring you've at the very least got a name and one direct contact method.

Ideally what we hope to find are contact details in one of three areas:

Marketing Contacts

Earlier we discussed some of the reasons why a company would like to give you something for free, and a lot of these reasons boil down to brand exposure.

Giving you a free product can result in you showing others the benefits of the product. With our book club example, all of the people in the club are seeing a new book and having exposure to the brand. As a marketing tool this is very effective, and something it's very hard for the company to replicate without spending a lot of money.

Therefore this type of contact is ideal when you need to find someone that has a lot of say in who gets given free products from the company.

PR Agencies

Not all companies do their marketing in house, and a lot will outsource this element of their business to a third party, or more specifically a PR agency. These agencies differ a little from typical marketing departments as they will promote the products of multiple brands. They are therefore very useful as contacts.

I'll talk a little more about PR agencies later in the book, but for now if you can find a PR agency contact, they are always the best person to speak to for a given company. Their sole role is to get exposure for a product, making them incredibly receptive to what you have to say.

Cold-calling PR agencies is very difficult too, so having a named contact within the agency is a godsend. Be sure to pull as much information as you can.

Sales

Companies may also want to give you something for free if it makes you more likely to try their product again in the future. This falls under the remit of the sales team rather than the marketing department, as it is their role to encourage sales and to maintain a healthy relationship with prospective customers.

So if we go back to our example of my desire to try other cheeses, this is far better suited to the sales team, as I am a prospective customer that would like to buy more from the brand in the future.

Sales contacts aren't quite as useful as marketing, because they often have short-term targets which can lead to less focus on the bigger picture – but that doesn't mean they can't be effective if you reach the right type of person.

Fleshing Out the Details

If you can't find anyone to contact, that makes things harder, as cold-calling/emailing is far more likely to be ignored than contact from someone who has done their research. The more you know about a company and their contacts the better, and the more chance of success you will have.

This is the logic behind the comments column for contacts, which will allow you to flesh out a back-story about that specific person, giving you more information to play with and build a rapport before you hit send.

As with the company search, there are a few questions you should seek to find information for:

- Are they the only person in that role?
- What is their job title?
- Do they have other activities online (e.g. a blog?)

You can find most of this information simply by typing their name into a search engine and seeing what comes up. Doing this may also bring up some profiles that person has online, such as social networking accounts on Facebook or LinkedIn. Make a note of these sites too, as they can be useful alternate methods for making contact with that specific individual in the future.

You could choose to ignore all of these steps and call a company directly. Then you'll need to ask to speak to their sales, marketing or PR departments. If all else fails this can work, but it's so much easier if you can ask to speak to Mr. X and then start talking to him about your offer.

Even walking into a retail store you'll find things a lot easier this way, and save yourself time in case the person you want to see is out or works in a completely different place.

The above steps for finding a company and a contact needn't be a lot of work either. Finding a company's website takes seconds online, and the contact details will either be listed under Contacts or Press Area. For five minutes of preparation you'll save yourself hours, and countless rejection emails later on.

P.S. I'm not a sales person, so can confirm there's no shame in finding a direct email address for someone and never speaking to them on the phone. If you're shy, this research will make it far easier when you do make contact, and give you extra confidence that what you are saying is right.

chapter 7

The Persona

Celebrities get products for free because of their personalities. They exude certain qualities that give companies the confidence anything given to them is likely to result in exposure or extra sales.

As members of the public we can emulate this, without the need to splash ourselves across glossy magazines, or to engage in any sort of scandal. We do this by creating a "persona".

This is one of the most fun steps in the process, and something you'll need to do before creating your offer for free stuff. It's what separates your approach from someone who appears rude and greedy by asking for freebies. It gives you confidence and a mask to hide behind, so any rejections can be brushed off and you can focus your energies on the successes.

What Is a Persona?

A "persona" is a slightly improved version of yourself. All of the doubts you have about yourself are hidden behind the persona, and your positive characteristics are brought to the fore. What's more, you only need to use the persona when making contact with companies, and can switch back to your normal self as soon as you hang up the phone.

What a persona won't do is give you a licence to lie or trick a company into sending you their product with you providing nothing in return. For that option I suggest becoming a con artist, and putting the book down now as that's not a long-term strategy for anyone.

Right, all the scammers gone?

Then I'll teach you how to craft your own persona:

1) Find Someone Who Inspires You

This could be a celebrity, a public figure, a CEO, or your best friend – anyone who seems confident or able to convince other people that what they have to say is worthwhile.

2) Discover Their Secret

People listen to others for a reason. You are reading this book because you trust me. You may have voted for a politician because you relate to them, or perhaps you found a salesman trustworthy because they were attractive. Whatever the reason, we are drawn to certain people, and what they say affects us in different ways.

What we want to do is emulate the best characteristics of our inspiring figure. To do this, we must ask a few questions:

- Where do they get their confidence?
- Where do they get their charisma?
- Why would someone listen to them?
- Would you like them if you met them?
- What makes them special?

■ What do they offer people?
■ How do they speak or write?

Once you've cracked those questions, you'll have a far greater understanding of what makes that person tick, and the characteristics you will need to borrow.

3) Add a Personal Touch

We are trying to borrow characteristics from other people but don't want to become them 100%. If it becomes apparent you are pretending to be someone, especially a famous person, then your chance of success lowers.

So you'll need to add a personal touch that reminds you of your persona but doesn't make it look like you are them. In my case, I have always liked the look of modern CEO's who go to work in polo-neck jumpers and have a high confidence about them. Therefore when I created my own persona I tried to emulate this by wearing a polo-neck jumper and mimicking their characteristics.

Whenever I wanted to become the "persona" I would put on the jumper and this reminded me of the elements that I needed to borrow.

I first tried this out by attending a trade show and found it incredibly liberating. The majority of people were wearing suits, and having the jumper made me stand out a little more. In my mind this helped me feel I was different and gave me the confidence to boldly walk up to companies and ask them point blank for their products.

You can emulate this in whichever way you wish. Clothing is just one idea, but you could also slightly change your accent, try to stand taller, walk differently, or make eye contact more often. It can be a minor change too. Even wearing a ring on a different finger could be the change you need to remind yourself to employ the characteristics of your new persona.

4) Try It On Yourself

Now we've identified the winning characteristics, we need to check if they work. Even the shy among us can do this, and hopefully feel empowered by the process. Grab a mirror, pick the characteristic you want to use and try it out. Talk to yourself and practise accordingly.

This will seem silly, but if you want to contact companies in any form that involves conversation, it's important to iron out the kinks first. If you'd rather write letters and emails, then put pen to paper and see if you can try to write in a way the other person would.

5) Try It On Others

After you feel ready, try the persona out on friends and family. Pretend that you're trying out a comedy routine and that this is simply your character. Clearly you don't want people to laugh, so explain you are trying to build your confidence and ask the gathered attendees to rate your "performance".

Over time you can ask your friends to try and catch you out, or ask you questions that a company might ask. For example:

- Why should we give something to you over everyone else?
- What can you offer us?
- Why do you need to speak to Mr. X?
- Will we get the product back?

It's better if they come up with their own ideas too, as you'll find it easier to think on your feet in a real conversation, so ask them to use the above as a guide, and to have fun. If done right this is a good learning exercise for both you and the friend asking questions. You may even find it gives you more confidence day to day.

If writing an email, then ask them to read it back, or have a role-play where they pretend to be a company and ask you questions in return. They'll also be learning the techniques in this book simply by playing the game with you, so they should get something out of the process as well.

Why the Persona Works

If you're a sceptic this may seem a little bit "New Age", or too much like a self-help book, but it's important to remember that we've all been through a similar process to the above in our childhood.

Who hasn't looked at other people and dreamed of one day becoming like them? We are all slightly different today than we were five years ago, and you only have to spend thirty minutes in a room with someone you admire to find yourself picking up some of their habits.

Ever started a new job and found yourself saying words and phrases you've never said before? That's your mind processing the things it likes from the world around it and feeding them back into your personality. We are always evolving ourselves and our "personas", so creating a new one for this purpose isn't a far stretch of the imagination.

As I've alluded to above, I am shy by nature, and this "persona" process tied in to my own change from geeky teenager to young adult, as I moved from glasses to contact lenses and messy hair to styled hair.

We also undergo personality changes, and using a "persona" is no different from the many changes we go through in our life, from child to teenager to young adult to family life. No matter where you are in your own life, you have already been through this process, and have an inbuilt capability to adapt.

When you're finished testing your persona, you can then remove the personal touch and go back to being yourself. If you like some of the aspects you've discovered over the way, it's fine to include them in your normal life. You can improve the persona over time – or if you choose one that doesn't work, change it altogether.

chapter 8

The Unique Offer

Now things get interesting. So far you've discovered the importance of bartering, that companies do want you to have their products for free, and a way to exude confidence when contacting companies. You also know the best person to contact in any company, and how to identify the products you want for free.

You've also heard me use the word "offer" a lot with regard to contacting companies, and this chapter will explain exactly what you can offer companies in return for their products. Then we'll branch off into numerous examples, to give you a really good range of tools.

You can use a single method for every company you contact, spending five minutes of preparation, or identify a few tools and blend them together into one unique solution. This chapter will prepare you for whatever you want to do – and whether you have loads of free time or want something to do in your lunch break, there will be a solution for you.

What Is a Unique Offer?

This chapter is all about the "unique offer", which is based on the business philosophy that every company needs a USP – Unique Selling Point. The logic is that no one will want to buy a product that is exactly the same as another product.

The process we use is exactly the same. If all you can offer is something a company already has, or a carbon copy of something else, you are far less attractive than someone who brings something new to the table.

Thankfully, the means detailed in this book are unique and open to personal interpretation. If I suggest you start a campaign to decide on the number one product of a particular type, one person might try to find the number one British film, asking for films to review so they can find the best – that's unique. Other readers may decide to do a totally different campaign for a different product, making the strategy the same, but the results different.

The other good news is that a lot of these ideas I've tried or seen used, so there's a good chance of success. But first, a little background on why you need the unique offer and the alternate.

When I first started, I sent letters to companies asking for free products, offering nothing in return. It was cheeky, I was somewhat naive, and fundamentally the success rate was very low. Most of the products I received were of little value – and based on the number of rejections I received, I wasted a lot of time writing letters and emails to discover that something-for-nothing really isn't an idea that stands up.

So linking back to our goal of bringing back bartering, we need to think instead about what we as individuals can offer the companies we contact. This could be any number of things. Here are just a few ideas on individual qualities we have that can tie in to this process:

Unique Offer – Day Job

Whatever you do in your day-to-day life, there may be a way you can link it to the process without getting fired.

You could offer a day of your time in return for a product, or a day of someone else's time. If you work for a company that sells a service, this is an ideal way to create a link between the two.

You'll need approval from your boss, and this is a far easier strategy if you're self employed, but it's certainly not an impossible proposition.

Example

Let's run this through an example. Jeff is a journalist who writes a weekly column about the local community. He only works for a small paper and has good relationships locally. Recently he's started to run out of ideas for the column and at the same time has a new baby on the way, so is stressed he won't be able to deliver the right articles with his time devoted to the new arrival.

What Jeff doesn't realise is he is already in an excellent position, as he has a platform to promote stuff he is given for free. However, he is also well trusted in the community, and therefore does not want to lose his editorial integrity. This is important, as if Jeff is seen to be writing only positive comments about free products it will ruin his reputation as a journalist.

Jeff finds himself with a unique offer in plain view: he can change his column to talk about fatherhood, and along the way he can discuss some of the products he receives.

This is fantastic brand exposure, as having a journalist talk about your product will always go down well. It's also ideal timing for Jeff, as he can change his outdated column into something new, and work it around the events occurring in this life, so it'll be convenient.

It's also a very unique offer, as not many journalists will be writing similar things, especially in the local area. Once Jeff identifies this, he can discuss the idea with his boss. The issue of editorial integrity can be resolved if Jeff is always honest about the products. If he hates a product he can tell the truth about it, and if the company makes a fuss he can give it back.

Jeff isn't being encouraged to lie or twist the truth. He gets the chance to retain his status within the local area, and the products he likes get seen by a new audience. His boss is aware of what he is doing, so there's no corporate trickery either.

Checklist

This is just one isolated example but there are common themes throughout. Use the following checklist to see if you can use your day job for free stuff:

1   Does the company provide a service you can offer people, or a product you can legally give away?

2   Do you have a good relationship with your boss, so that they would agree to something like this?

3   Does accepting free products potentially disrupt your job role or create a conflict of interest?

4   Would it disrupt your day job to the point of you being distracted and more focused on freebies than the job at hand?

Answered yes to 1 and 2 and no to 3 and 4? Then you've passed, and all that remains is for you to write down your offer. This should be a single paragraph, short enough that a company can understand exactly what you are offering quickly.

The Unique Offer

For Jeff, his offer would read as follows:

"I am creating a column which reviews baby products, and am looking for products to test. This will appear in the X Newspaper seen by an audience of 20,000 daily readers."

It's simple and to the point, with a clear benefit for the company involved. What about if the offer was something a bit more out there? Let's imagine a scenario where a teenage boy has a cleaning service. He cleans houses and offices in his spare time, and wants to get some parts for his car for free. His offer would be more like:

"I am a professional cleaning firm looking to offer my services in return for car parts. My services have been used by <company names> and recommended by <company name>."

This example is a little forward, and can only be used for a particular product in specific places (e.g. garages, car dealerships), but it does the job. Again, it's clear, and explains what he wants and what he is offering in return. The second sentence gives recommendations and makes the offer more legitimate and likely to be respected by those who receive it.

Link It to the Persona

The "persona" comes into play here too, with the word "professional". This is one of these interesting words that doesn't need any validation other than the fact you are using it. If you are proud of your company services, you can call yourself professional, but everyone else could hate the company.

In this case we've convinced ourselves that our services are the best, and this comes across in the unique offer within the first sentence, "professional cleaning service". At no point does this sound like the work of an amateur cleaning service run in a college student's spare time. It sounds like a real company, and therefore will be taken more seriously than an email clearly sent from a college student.

If you can't pass the earlier questions then this isn't the idea for you (but that's OK as there are plenty more). This is a great concept if you have the potential, and in many ways is how a lot of small businesses survive when they are starting out. Nowhere is the idea of bartering more alive than in small businesses, and we could clearly learn a lot from their tactics.

10 Day Job Unique Offer Examples

- An accountant offering to do the taxes of every restaurant in town to get a free lunch from each one.
- A florist offering free flowers to a wedding cake company, if they offer free cakes in return for her customers.
- A hairdresser who will cut the hair of every team member in an office in return for free signage.
- A company offering a free car to anyone who will manage their marketing for a year.
- An oven company giving a pizza oven away in return for free pizza any time they want.

- A woman requesting free makeup for her office in return for everyone trying the product.
- A children's hospital asking for free toys that will then be played with by countless children.
- Local cinemas giving away free tickets to all businesses within five miles in the hope they'll come again.
- Free driving lessons to all people referred by a school.
- Free parking if an office has spare spaces, in return for services from those who park there.

Unique Offer – Blogging

If you don't have a day job that fits in with the previous chapter's strategies, then you can always create a new part-time job that does. This doesn't need to be an extensive time drain, and the best way to create this is through a free blog, giving you no costs in case you change your mind.

Jeff wrote a newspaper column to get free stuff for his newborn baby, but let's imagine we like writing but don't have an outlet to share what we write. That's where blogging comes into play. Anyone can create a blog online in a matter of minutes, without a single credit-card payment.

An Internet search for "free blog" will give you numerous examples, and it's easy to find websites that have been created purely for the purpose of talking about anything they get for free.

Example (My Favourite Strategy)

I can personally vouch for this as a means of getting stuff for free as it's how I first started out. The first product I ever received for free was a video game, simply because I had written a website about the topic.

I would never have expected the product for free and it was only through chance that a writer offered to help out with the site and asked me if I'd ever had any free games. At the time the concept of free stuff was unknown to me, and companies then were far less likely to give stuff away than they are now.

Despite this her words intrigued me and so I wrote down an offer along the lines of:

"We are a leading video game website read by 1,000 visitors a day, looking for new games to review. If you have anything of interest we would be happy to feature it."

By the time I finished the site two years later I had received over 200 video games for free. Many of these came from the same companies, whom I only needed to convince once in order to receive a continuing flow of free stuff.

This symbolises two things. The first is that it is very possible to get products simply by promising to talk about them, and the second is that having a blog is a valid enough place to talk about these products.

To see if this worked for more than just video games, I set up a new website that promised to review anything I was sent. The success was repeated with everything from designer trainers to kitchen sinks sent my way. I reviewed everything I was sent on a free blog, and the story got picked up by newspapers around the globe.

A simple blog can work wonders, and I found my best success came from the times I tried to offer something which no other site did (which led to the "unique offer" concept). So if I tried to request a product for review that wasn't normally reviewed, I could expect a very high success rate.

Ironing Board Reviews?

Start a website about ironing-board covers and you're likely to be successful almost every time. I've never found a website that reviews them, and yet the companies who make them are just as keen on having their products exposed as any other company.

Finding an under-represented product that you can talk about is an ideal scenario. The best way to do this is to decide what you'd like for free and search for it with the word "review" afterwards. Search for "video game reviews" and you'll find a lot of options to compete with. Try "Ironing board reviews" and suddenly the potential market shrinks, and you have discovered an interesting blogging opportunity that companies will be receptive to.

There's no reason just to limit yourself to the one area you search for. So if you want a free ironing-board cover, you can create a blog about products for the home and turn it into a site that reviews any such items you are sent for free. This will make the project more fun for you, while still giving you the opportunity to approach those desperate ironing-board cover manufacturers.

Remember how we picked a category of products that we'd like earlier on? Well, that could be the starting topic of your blog. Find a free blog and create your site around the topic, making sure to add your own contact details so companies can contact you easily. You also want to attract the passing companies who like your site and want to be involved.

You'll need some content before contacting companies, so pick items you already own and write as much as you can about them. Share your experiences and try to discover your writing style. You'll find it far easier to talk about any products you are sent, and may even get a bit of website traffic that you can speak about when first contacting the companies.

After you're happy with what you've written, share the website with your friends and ask them to spread the word. Over time, having good content will also see you picked up by the search engines, helping improve the target audience of your site no end.

Be sure to make it clear you review products that are sent to you by adding a statement to that effect on every page, but don't include your postal address at this stage – just an email address is fine.

The Unique Offer

If you've got that all written up, then it's time to contact companies and to sum up your offer. Most likely this will be:

"I am the editor of a blog that reviews <Product Type>. We have featured products from <Brands> and are looking for new products to review. Please contact me on the details below if you have anything of interest."

In the brands section, just include the names of brands you already own and have talked about. The aim is to show that some of their competitors have been featured, but not to lie and say they have actually sent you their products.

Link It Back to the Persona

The "persona" is popping in again, this time with the labelling of ourselves as "editors". Like the term "professional", this is an easy label to apply that is truthful but makes us seem better than we actually are.

Clearly, as it is your blog you are the editor (and also the writer, marketer, customer support, technical support and HR person), but seeing this written down makes the site seem bigger than it actually is. This is just the sort of image we need to portray when competing with bigger sites that have been reviewing products for years.

Calling yourself a "journalist" is just as easy, and I've attended countless conferences and events as a "senior journalist". This was 100% factual as I was senior (i.e. the longest serving) and also a journalist (i.e. I wrote about things), so it created an inflated sense of importance. In reality I was one of a team of three writers, all reviewing games in our spare time, all desperate to get stuff for free. But the job title sounds good and makes people feel confident on hearing it that they are speaking to the right person.

So whether you call yourself an editor, senior journalist or managing director, the important thing is to establish that you are the most important person they need to speak to.

Over time you will find the blog grows, and through writing good content the number of people arriving on the site should increase. You can still spend 20 minutes every few days writing content, or may even find it grows into a strong side project you can sell advertising space on. Not bad for a gimmick dedicated to getting free products!

10 Blogging Unique Offer Examples

- A website that reviews local attractions.
- A blog focused on how well shoes fit, which tests any shoes that are sent.

- A giant calendar focused on forthcoming events, which links to comments on each event.
- A summary of unusual products you find online, with reviews of those you are sent.
- A cosmetics blog that tries out every product sent.
- A news blog, focused on new companies in the local area, which gets invited to try their wares.
- A travel blog which will try any hotel and talk about it.
- A blog connecting mothers together to share their opinions on children's toys.
- A top 10 video games website, which tries all new games and may or may not add them to their top 10.
- A sports news site that will cover any sporting event they are given free tickets to.

Unique Offer – Photos

Like the idea of blogging but not very good at writing? Then using photos as your unique offer is another excellent solution.

Just like blogging, there are numerous websites that let you share photos for free (search for "free photo sharing" to find them). You can also do this offline by submitting photos to photography magazines, local newspapers or in a gallery. Our goal is the same: free products.

There are two potential versions of this offer:

Unique Offer #1: Photos Using Products

If you wrote earlier that you'd like some free photographic equipment, then this is the solution for you. By taking lots of photos on different photographic equipment you are encouraging companies to send you free products and compete against one another to see whose product is best. This is similar to writing reviews, except the pictures do the talking, and as you test each product the review is actually writing itself.

You don't necessarily need to be an expert photographer to go down this route. I've suggested this for both students on photography courses and people who take one photo a year – the core principle is to try different products in different uses. For a company, being able to prove their product can be used by professionals and the public is very important, as both markets play a key role in their sales.

If you decide this is the strategy for you, you'll need photos taken on different cameras. Even if you don't have access to many different pieces of kit, borrow a camera from a friend, take a picture and give it back.

Log all the pictures on your chosen outlet and be sure to include details about the product the picture was taken on. If you can include information on other aspects such as lens sizes, and any effects used, this will help to create a more professional persona.

You can then approach companies offering to try out their products and take pictures with them for inclusion on your outlet. The photos don't need to be of exotic landmarks either. Simply take photos that appeal to you and try to show something in a different way to others (either with filters, interesting angles, or subject matter that is unique).

Unique Offer #2: Photos of Products

The alternate strategy is to use whichever camera you have lying around and take photos of products in interesting ways. When I got a crate of energy drink for free, a group of guys tried to get one as well by building a tower out of their leftover cans and taking a photo to send to the manufacturer. This showed great brand loyalty on their part, and was rewarded with a free crate of the product.

Their offer was certainly unique, and there are similar ways this could be done for any product, even if you don't actually buy the product in the first place. You don't even need a camera. You can grab a product image off the Internet, make a few tweaks to it and post it online for everyone to talk about. The more funny and unique you can make the image, the better. Your goal is simply to create something that stands out when placed next to the normal product image and attracts attention.

Once you've taken your photo, or edited your image, you can send this to the manufacturer (or their competitor) and ask for some free product for another photo you are doing. This should be the logical evolution of your original photo idea (so if you took photos of a tower of drinks cans, explain you want to make a bigger one or set a world record – but more on that later).

Once you've had free products from one company you can twist the idea and go to another company, or try something entirely different, making sure to reference your previous photo when asked what photos you have taken.

You don't have to be an amazing photographer to use this approach, or have an eye for detail. What's more important here is the ability to think outside the box, and to do something a typical photographer wouldn't do. It's rare for a company to market their product with weird photography, but they are certainly receptive to the idea; and in so far as providing a unique way to promote their product, it's one of the most original ideas out there.

10 Photography Unique Offer Examples

- A gallery exhibition comprising the same photo on multiple camera setups.
- An edited image to show lots of different brands fighting, with one emerging the victor.
- A simple photo of you holding your favourite product of that day up to the camera and smiling.
- An online photo gallery with free flowers you have grown.
- A photo blog focused on brands you saw that day.
- An exercise guide, with photos of you on different equipment.
- An around-the-world journal that includes photos of places that have given you free stuff along the way.
- Pictures of soup (it worked for Andy Warhol!)
- Get invited to factories and take pictures.
- A website that reviews cameras, where the author takes photos of him/herself in the mirror holding each camera (the ultimate faux pas photo shot).

Unique Offer – Videos

If you can't write and hate photography, then videos are the logical next step to try. In many ways they offer a superior means, because people are more inclined to share videos than any other type of online media. This makes them the most powerful tool if you want to reach companies and wow them with the response.

Example #1

Two corporate students in America, Chris Barrett and Luke Mccabe, put this to the test in excellent fashion by becoming the first corporately sponsored students in America. Their tuition and many of the possessions they had during their time at university were paid for by companies. In return, they shot videos of themselves using the products and distributed these to media outlets in America.

As Chris and Luke have done this idea it's no longer unique, in America at least, but the principles of what they did make it an excellent case study in how simple video projects can be used to meet our goals.

The Unique Offer

Like the blog and photo projects, our main goal here is product exposure and being able to receive free products in return for the role we play in showing these products to the masses.

The format of video makes this is a much easier project to start and change than any other. You can make a complicated video showing a product from multiple angles in different uses, or stick the camera in your face and talk about why you love product X.

As with everything in this book, the amount of effort you put in is likely to translate into the relative reward. In addition, you may want to involve friends in the process, as their creative input (not to mention having one person to hold the camera while you chat to it) can be a real help in passing ideas around.

If you choose to go down this road you should watch out for negative comments, as anything that seems overly promotional is likely to be harshly commented on by the online community.

Example #2

So for your first video, rather than going on and on about how much you love product X, try to find a unique way to turn a hobby into a video.

For example, Jenna loves skateboarding and wants to get free equipment from the big manufacturers. Her friends feel she could be a rising star, but she doesn't have the money to attend the major tournaments.

What Jenna could do is have her friends film videos of her skating and post these online. If she is as good as her friends think she is, then people are likely to share the videos – and as the skating community is very active online, the companies who live in this world are likely to find her video.

If this isn't working fast enough, she can film a video of her testing products to breaking point. Her unique offer could be that "she will try any product until it breaks" and she can use this to go direct to companies once she has a few example videos in the bag.

Over time Jenna may even be able to attract a corporate sponsor if she allows this relationship to grow. This will allow her to enter the major tournaments, and the power of free stuff will turn into a true monetary value.

It's a very specific example, but the important thing to consider is that video is the perfect form for Jenna. Testing products until they break has no effect in written words, and photos will only tell half the story.

Tie It Back to the Persona

You should consider this and the persona when deciding on your own medium of choice. Should your persona have lots of confidence and make people laugh, videos are perfect. If all you want to do it talk to the camera about products that's fine, but you should also consider doing this with a blog. If you want to film a video of a really cool item that doesn't move, you should consider if photos will do the job just as well.

This is all part of having a blended strategy. One week you may find photos do the trick, and another week a video may be the best way to contact a different company.

Don't be afraid to try video marketing as one way of getting your name out there. Perhaps you've set up a blog reviewing cosmetic products and need to get exposure. A video of you trying the products out will help draw people to the main blog. You've strengthened your unique offer by making it easier for people to find the blog and have a higher chance of getting products.

10 Video Unique Offer Examples

- Be a guinea pig for a day and test any product.
- Film yourself struggling to perform a menial task and ask for a better solution.
- Posts videos of your pets and ask for products for them to try.
- Offer to wear a tee-shirt with a company's logo all day and film the results.
- Walk into shops asking for free stuff, with a camera behind you. This is more effective than no camera.
- Create a viral campaign to promote a product.
- Talk to the camera about why a product is rubbish and what they could do to improve it.
- Write a song about a product and sing it to the camera.
- Try and use a typical product in an unusual way.
- Talk about your unique offer (for any other of the ideas in this book) and film a video that explains it.

Unique Offer – Friends

Sure, friends aren't very unique – we've all got one good friend, or at the very least work colleagues – but the methods in which we connect with our friends are very different. We all have friends of different interests, and let's face it companies are far more interested in convincing multiple people to try their products than just one. So this is where the social aspect comes into play.

I've focused a fair bit on online activities for the last few chapters because there are so many great things online that you can set up for free. Thankfully, friends are something you can set up for free that can be done without even having an Internet connection.

First, take a piece of paper and write down all the friends you have. It doesn't have to be hundreds; even a handful will suffice. Then in the next column write down their likes and dislikes. When you're done, try to group people together, so everyone who likes one product is in group A and everyone who likes another is in group B (not literally – this will be fine on the paper).

The Unique Offer

With that in place, you've created a pool of potential fans of different products which can then be used as an offer. For example:

"My friends and I have been lifelong fans of mountain biking and want to try some new equipment. We spend hundreds every year on new kit and want to try a new brand. Do you have any old display samples we can try and share with our friends?"

What the example does is create a need for a company to fill. Sure, companies could pay thousands of pounds outsourcing their market research to nameless individuals, or they could hire a keen bunch of volunteers who have made the effort to contact them.

All we are doing with this type of strategy is using friends as a marketing tool. There's no friend manipulation, and if anything they stand to see the benefits of the products that are received.

It's important to remember that when we turn to some of the online applications of this strategy and take a look at social networks. Sites like Facebook, MySpace and Twitter give us instant access to our friends, and a simple and effective way to see how many we have and contact them one by one.

Tie It Back to the Persona

Like our example on the piece of paper, we can still group our friends into likes (most social networks even do this for you with shared interest options) and get a good understanding of the number of people that would like a specific product. We can even look at their personas and how these can fit together. Better to form a group of friends with complementary personas than one that seems unlikely to mesh together.

Better still, companies are dying to find ways to make contact with people on these websites without seeming spammy. Therefore if you can utilise your friend list and expose a product while still coming across as honest, you've delivered a marketing dream.

The best way to do this is approach companies offering to discuss their product with a certain number of people. This could be everyone on your friends list, or a group that you start on the social sites. Either way the end goal is the same, to ignite debate over a product – a debate that you can fuel by discussing the products you are sent for free.

Example

If we take our mountain biking example, we can pool the same group of friends together online and this time create a group on a social media site called "Mountain Bike Testers".

We'll then send the message round to other friends, try to get them to join and ask them to invite other people that have shared passions. Eventually we'll have grown our group of friends into a much larger network of people, all still connected.

Now if we approach a company asking for a product to test there's a much stronger potential audience.

There's also a specific site we can talk about their product – and because social media sites accept photo and video content, we can choose to talk about the product in any way we want.

As the group wasn't created on the premise of everyone getting free stuff, only the original members need receive the product. Although you can always encourage other group members to talk about their own experiences, or even try to get free stuff themselves. Why not share the free stuff love?

10 Friends Unique Offer Examples

- Offer to email everyone on your friend list a special offer if the company gives you something for free.
- Advertise on a social networking website you'll test anything you get given.
- Follow people on Twitter who have similar interests. Then share your resources to get freebies.
- Start a group asking for the best tips on free things and share your knowledge with others.

- Create a career profile on LinkedIn and try to use your job as a means of bartering.
- Join online groups about products, become an active member of the community, and offer to write about products on there.
- Find companies on social networks. Offer to become an ambassador of their product and spread the word.
- Ask your friends what they have received for free. Then try to do a similar thing yourself.
- Stand in town asking people if they want stuff for free. Then work together to achieve this.
- Record a song about your favourite products. List it on a social network and send it to companies.

Unique Offer – Clubs and Groups

One of the first examples in this guide was to start a club talking about products and then to approach companies asking for stuff to talk about. I used this example because it's one of the simplest to understand, and also the most low-tech. You just need a few friends, a front room and a topic to discuss.

It's also a relatively under-used concept. Sure, people get together and chat about books, movies and TV, but in terms of asking companies for products to talk about that's a golden opportunity, and one countless groups and clubs are missing out on every day.

Example

But first, let's assume you have no club and are starting the process from scratch. You'll first need something to talk about. As with our friends topic, this can be done simply by splitting your friends into groups based on common interests and then trying to find a pool of friends whom you feel would be receptive to the idea. If you already chat to a group of friends about a particular topic then you're half-way there and simply need to formalise what you do.

Starting a group, or turning an existing set of conversations into a club, is very easy. In fact, you don't even need to pick a day to sit down and chat. If it just so happens you talk about films every couple of weeks already, then you're set. If you don't have regular chats, then start introducing the topic in conversation.

Ask friends about products they've used recently and relate stories of your own. Try to engage them as much as possible in this topic, and if you feel it isn't working try a different topic with a separate group of friends.

If this doesn't work either, you can always find some different friends, or place a free classified ad asking for people who are interested in the product type. Arrange a neutral place to meet (e.g. a bar instead of your house) and try to start the conversation flowing. If people are nervous, try to involve them. And if you aren't confident yourself, print off a list of questions everyone in the group should answer, and use this as a conversation starter instead.

When the group is formed and the common interest has been pinned down, you are ready to start critiquing the products you already have. Rather than jumping straight to free stuff, talking about things you own helps the group get used to commenting on products and sharing opinions. It doesn't cost anything as you'll already have the products to hand, and if one group member has something others don't then they can share this with the group – which is also a free way to try something new.

Now the group has confidence and a topic, you have the strength to turn this into a unique offer when contacting companies. The main power of the group is for word-of-mouth advertising. If one group member gets a film for free and loves it, they are likely to share this opinion with other members of the group, and this will probably lead to a purchase. That's great news for the sales and marketing departments of companies, and good news for whoever receives the free product.

Unique Offer

Knowing this trick, you'll need to construct a letter, email or phone call that summarises the following points:

- what the group does
- how many members you have (no big deal if only 5-10)
- how often you meet
- what other products you've discussed

We'll review contact methods in a lot more detail later on in the book, but for now this list will give you the selling points you need. If you can convince a company that your group has a good shared pool of experience and is a fit with their brand, then it's a natural step for them.

Tie It Back to the Persona

Over time, you can grow the group and make it an even stronger proposition. For the most part you will be doing all the contacting of companies and using your own persona to act as the sole face and head of the group. This doesn't always have to be the case, though.

The more members you have, the easier it will be for other group members to contact companies. You needn't restrict the contacting to just one person either. As people have been with the group for a while, or if you spot someone who has a confident persona, introduce them to the concepts in this book and ask them to get involved as well.

Once more people get freebies, they can be rotated across the group, and all members will benefit in the long run.

10 Clubs and Groups Unique Offer Examples

- A group of friends who compare their favourite movies and ask companies for new movies to try.
- A weekly meeting of new mothers that get together to discuss the best baby products.
- A group of students who ask for free entry into different clubs, so they can share the best ones with their friends.
- Five friends who love food ask restaurants if they can try one course for free. If they like it, there's a chance they'll pay for the whole meal.
- Local businesses who ask if they can try one another's products for free. They may then share the word with their own customers.
- A bunch of gamers who play online weekly ask for new products to try. If one gets a freebie, the others rent/buy the game to try it as well.
- A book author who wants real public opinion and asks her readers to form a group to review her new book.
- A charity gets its entire staff together and asks for free entry to an event to reward them for their hard work.
- An amazing ice skater asks for free entry to an ice rink, in return for showing off his talents to the people already there.

■ A cat rescue centre groups all its cats together (making them a club) and asks people to see them and adopt them for free – thereby making the product itself into the club and the free offer.

Unique Offer – Become an Expert

Following on from the club example, there's an alternate angle to consider and that comes from becoming such a strong group that companies actively seek you out to get your opinion. Rather than continually contacting companies, they will instead use you as a focus group, offering you products in return for your opinions.

Example

Film studios do this all the time when they host free preview screenings of big films. They invite a group of people along, grant them free entry, and then ask for questionnaires to be completed at the end of the film. This grants them public opinion for free, allowing them to tweak the film before release.

Or, in the case of movies that are previewed weeks before their main releases, it creates an early buzz around the film and starts word-of-mouth marketing.

Tie It Back to the Persona

Either way, it's effective and doesn't always need to be done as a group. This all comes back to the persona and what we choose to brand ourselves as. If you call yourself an expert in beauty products, it's not that much of a stretch for people to believe you.

If a company then believes in your expertise enough to send you something in return for your feedback, that's effective bartering of knowledge for a product.

The issue is how far we choose to push this. I could wake up tomorrow, call myself an expert in beauty products, and find I have absolutely nothing to say on the matter when a product turns up. In fact, the first time I got some beauty products for free, while running a different experiment, I had no idea what to say and had to ask my wife for her opinions instead.

There is therefore no point labelling yourself as an expert in something in which you have no interest. Likewise, if you choose to lie excessively in this approach you will find yourself stuck for words and probably having to give the product back (or at least be blacklisted from any others).

Unique Offer

So let's be sensible here and have a think about what we really know. If you were on Mastermind tomorrow, what would your specialist subject be? If it links to something you know at work, that's great. Perhaps there's a product you've always had a passion for, or you already read a magazine on a topic. These aspects alone don't make you an expert, but they're enough of a starting point to at least explore this possibility.

When you've got a rough idea what you want to go for, it's then a case of positioning yourself and trying to gain a reputation as an authoritative source on the subject. You need people to see the knowledge you have and genuinely believe you possess unique knowledge on the topic.

As with all so-called "gurus" on a topic, this knowledge that you have can be a shared collection of other people's opinions and things you have read online. So long as you have your own opinions on a topic and a passion for something, it's very easy to read other blogs, newspaper stories and magazines about the subject, digest all this information, and gain a reputation as being an expert.

To get this reputation known, alongside reading all this information, you should try to ignite debate on each topic. So if someone expresses a strong opinion about a new range of clothes, you hit back with comments to their article that reflect your own opinion. If there's a review you don't agree with, then make it known you have strong opinions the other way.

This strategy on its own won't work, and it's where many of the earlier tools come into play. Start a blog collecting your knowledge on a topic, film videos expressing your opinions and criticising others, or take photos of the things you have expertise on. There's no reason to become a hated figure or deliberately rip others to shreds – but if you can create a healthy debate around topics in a product category, then eventually you will get noticed.

So how do you know if you've been noticed? Well, people in the communities you frequent will start to comment more on your posts, and if your email address is available you'll start to receive questions through email and private messages. These messages may not straight away be about free products, but you can help encourage this possibility. To do so, start writing the following types of posts:

- challenges for companies (e.g. can anyone make a better product than X)
- requests for products to review
- criticisms of products with notes on how they could be better

All of these types of conversation can be created on blogs, forums, in videos or as letters to your local paper. They cost nothing to do, and you can talk about products you already own.

This is one of the few strategies where you can get freebies without ever actually contacting a company. The goal is to get them to contact you by saying things that act as the bait. So rather than spending time sending out emails you can focus on writing interesting things and facilitating debate between customers of a product.

The last thing to consider is that you shouldn't go over the top with negative comments. If you need to criticise a product that's fine, but make sure all your comments can be backed up with fact. If a film is too short, that's fine as it's a fact. However, if you say a product is rubbish because it was made by monkeys, you run the risk of problems if that can't later be proven.

Thankfully, it's fairly easy to tell the difference between fact and fiction, and even if you need to express a strong hatred for a product, so long as it is your own opinion it will be fine. After all, an opinion is just that, and no one can tell you whether you should or shouldn't enjoy a product.

10 "Expert" Unique Offer Examples

- Complain that all DVD players should have built in karaoke facilities, and ask a company to create an effective combination of the two.
- Write a list of tips a company should use when making their next product, then ask other people to comment on them.
- Film a video stating you want to find the best book on the market and that you'll read anything.
- Review anything and everything you can get your hands on.
- Call the local paper and ask if you can write an article on the hotels you have stayed in. This may lead to offers to try out others.
- If you've got a comment on how a company can make something better, send it in to them. You may be rewarded.
- If you made a group (e.g. a movie club) then get the group to list how to make a perfect product. Send this back with your comments on the freebies you get.
- Sign up for any testing websites. They'll send you products in return for comments. Don't pay them any money, and read up on them first.
- Start writing on a voucher forum about why a company should give their product away. You may even convince them to do so.
- Walk into local businesses, tell them your expertise and that you'd like to give them a day of your time to help them. All you want in return is some free products (you'll be much cheaper than a consultant).

Unique Offer – Charity

This is by far the number one request that I receive for help – which is madness when you think about it. By their very nature charities are designed for free stuff. People devote their time and energies for free, in an effort to help people, and in many cases the only way they can do this is if they are given free money or free products.

As what they are doing is helping a good cause, this should in many ways be a good enough offer to convince companies to send them stuff. Sadly, for various reasons, many companies don't interact with charities or simply have their hands tied from a legal perspective.

Thankfully, with a little bit of ingenuity it is possible to play on some of the strengths that charities have in order to get companies to listen. For example, charities are in a fantastic position to engage with the media. Flick through any local paper and charities often dominate the headlines with how much they've raised or how many people they've helped. Any time a company makes a decent-sized donation this is also included, giving the company exposure and helping their brand.

In addition charities are great at engaging people and convincing members of the public to support what they are doing. This creates a network of people ready to push the unique offer forward and spread the good word. It also creates exposure for the work the charity is doing, as any donations they receive are known to these members.

So, by this logic, charities can use their ability to attract attention (both in the media and public) as a selling point, and to entice companies in with the possible brand exposure they will receive.

Sadly, this approach isn't for everyone. I am in no way encouraging setting up charities just to get free things. As with the entire book, no con artists need apply here. You'll also find companies consider the charity angle a lot more seriously if your charity has a registered charity number.

Tie It Back to the Persona

For charities their persona is very much defined already. It will be based around their mission statement, whether that be fighting a disease or saving kittens. The persona will already have an element of helping the community, and this will come across as a strong selling point when you talk to people.

You'll also find that the tone that needs to be used when communicating should do all it can to make people trust that what you are doing is right and unique. People may be sceptical if you want free products to support a small charity which is identical to a larger charity.

Unique Offer

Due to the above scepticism, simply being a charity isn't enough on its own. Every charity in the world will be competing for free products from companies, and therefore you need a unique hook to define your charity.

If you're a smaller version of an existing charity, then perhaps your offer is that you serve the local community better than the big players. Alternatively, if you tackle an issue no other charity does, then this is already a very strong offer in itself. Personal passion goes a long way too, and if you relate to a cause this will help people get on side.

Simply having a good charity isn't yet cause enough for freebies. On rare occasions you may find companies are cooperative because they want to be seen to do good, but for the most part you'll still need to convince them something is in it for them – a sad state of affairs, but almost always the case.

The best way to do this is to create a timed deadline. This will add urgency to the request and push those companies who may have waited weeks to donate (and then forgotten) into more immediate action.

What's more, if you can position the deadline to coincide with an event that has public and media exposure, there is a reward for any companies that take you up on your offer. In addition, if the event is a success you have improved awareness of your charity, making it easier to initiate contact with companies again in the future.
Example
I worked through these steps myself during my own charity crusade, so can prove that they are effective. Having received a lot of free products, and starting to run out of space in my home, I decided to give them away to a charity that helps provide clean water in poorer countries.

This in itself didn't seem like enough, and I wanted to see if companies would also join me and give away product samples they no longer needed. So I decided I would contact them as well.

In addition to this, I had agreed to give away my samples in an existing auction for the charity, meaning I didn't need to go through the process of creating an event or a deadline, as one was ready for me to use. So I contacted the organisers and arranged a place in the auction. They detailed my involvement on their website and this gave me a reference point for companies, to prove that what I was doing had the backing of a charity.

With these elements in place I had an offer that was quite appealing, a charity and a persona driven by my own desire to give away my freebies.

So I wrote emails to companies asking them to join me. Many got involved because they were impressed by the time and energy I put into the project (something true of everyone that works in a charity).

The other companies wanted to give products simply to get their names involved in the auction, or because I had built a relationship with them through previous free products (but more on relationships later).

All of the companies who gave were driven by the deadline, which was one month from the auction – just enough time to allow them to provide the finished products. A longer time period than this could have caused them to lose interest or to put off helping altogether.

The auction rolled around and was a great success. Over 300 people were in attendance, and the list of products given away was shown on the charity website. There was great brand exposure for the companies who helped, and I wrote to thank each and every one of them after the event, so they had feedback on what they helped achieve.

Although this is my experience, I hope it shows how the different elements can be swapped around for your charity, or event. An auction is by far and away the easiest option, as all you need is a hall and a few people to turn up. However, you could also invite members of the public to your charity base of operations to see how the products you receive help. This could be to see a new litter of kittens being fed, or to watch a video of feedback from lives you saved in Africa. Both events can be given a fixed time, and the products a deadline.

To get the public involved in your event, contact the local papers and leave free classified adverts wherever you can (both offline and online). You should also contact the council and get permission to put flyers up in your local town and on bulletin boards. You could also drop leaflets through doors or hand them out in the street. Can't afford leaflets? Then ask a local printer to do them in return for their logo appearing on every one.

The other angle to consider is that the products you receive can be used as donations to help the cause itself. From cat food to unused knickers, charities can use a remarkable amount of free things to help people. If this is the case, you should play on the mindset of companies who have stock they no longer need.

Contact local businesses and try to reach an arrangement where their unsold product is donated to help your cause. In return they can tell customers about the work they do with your charity, and this can build a long-term relationship between you both.

There are even more ways to get people to donate to your cause, as detailed below:

10 Charity Unique Offer Examples

- A kitten charity asks people to donate unwanted cat food.
- A local effort to save a landmark, holding an auction to raise funds.
- A school asks for toys for its younger students in return for brand exposure.
- A group of people band together to save their local pub, by staging an all-night lock-in and inviting people to buy donated products.
- A company gives away its ex-display products that it can't sell.
- A fast-food chain provides all its unsold food to the homeless each night.
- A zoo asks a garage to donate broken tyres, for their monkey enclosures.
- An artist asks people to donate paintings so he can hold a free gallery and provide exposure for new artists.
- A company sells its products to employees and then donates the profits to a charity.
- An author offers to write a novel about someone for free, in return for help with a charity project.

Unique Offer – Set a Record

Of all the types of offers this one is probably the most fun, and in going down this route you may even find setting the records more enjoyable than receiving the products.

The goal is to find a record which already exists and break it, or to create a new record and set the bar for others to beat. A quick search online for "set a world record" will give you plenty of places to apply, and you'll also find lots of existing records to either beat or use for inspiration just by searching for "world records".

Tie It Back to the Persona

The type of personality you'll want to use if trying to set a record is one of untold confidence. No matter what people say, you must believe that you can break the record. That doesn't mean you shouldn't research a record that you think you can break first, but thankfully there are lots of easy-to-beat records. This is simply because not that many people have attempted to break all the records, so you should be able to find something that at least looks possible.

When this is done, try to attempt a smaller version of the record, to give yourself confidence that you can beat it. While it won't be the end of the world if you don't break the record, your display of confidence is designed to inspire other people to help you and to get them to support you – especially if those people work for companies who supply a product that is necessary to break the record.

Unique Offer

This really is a logical extension of the unique offer, as you are setting yourself a goal that you want to achieve and asking for help from companies. The unique offer is the fact you want to break a record, and there's potential for any companies who help you to get exposure on the back of it.

A lot of records will require some type of product to be used. If you're attempting to do something in a hot-air balloon, you'll need someone to rent you one. Should you want to eat something in double-quick time, ask the manufacturer to get involved and donate the product.

What we want to do here is try and "wow" the company. Our confident persona will go some way to doing this, and we can also impress them with the record itself by trying to pick something inspiring or just a bit silly.

The unique offer doesn't just have to go to companies. A lot of TV shows, and websites, are dedicated to people breaking records, and will hold video demonstrations of these attempts. So try searching around online for such an opportunity and contact them with your offer. For the TV show/website they get more content, and they should provide the product you need for the record attempt.

Example

A phone-book company followed these steps, and recruited people to sit in the middle of a large shopping centre to attempt to break a record. These two volunteers were encased in a glass box each, and given a copy of the phone directory.

The record was for them to try and outdo each other by asking companies to give them products, which would then appear in their glass box. This exposed those products to any shoppers who happened to walk past. In addition they could only contact companies through the phone directory, as they couldn't leave the box – so the directory company had great exposure as well.

In the end the volunteers amassed a sizeable pile of freebies and could keep them when they emerged from their boxes.

This is a great example of a simple attempt to set a record evolving and offering product exposure for multiple companies. The record itself pales in comparison to the end results for everyone involved. It also attracted a fantastic media response, as journalists gathered to report on the event. Members of the public were also won over, because the people in the boxes were average Joes and not company employees.

I've also attempted to break records, including a challenge set to me by a radio station to get ten free products chosen by their listeners. My goal was to hunt down these products in a week and meet back at the studio to donate the products.

It was a very difficult challenge as these were specific products and brands, so if a company refused to cooperate this hampered the process. However, the products I did receive were mainly possible because I had the backing of the radio station.

My unique offer was that anything I got donated would be mentioned on the station to all their listeners. I made sure to hammer this fact home to everyone I contacted, quoting listener figures for the station and promoting their involvement.

The station itself held an interview with me initially when the readers proposed their choices, so this helped prove my involvement, and created a little bit of hype before I had even contacted the companies.

All of these elements worked in my favour, and most of the listeners got what they asked for. Even the DJ was given a free product, and one listener who had asked for a cuddly toy was given two.

10 Record Breaking Unique Offer Examples

- A man attempts to eat 10 cookies in a set time period.
- A woman wants to set the record for the most jumps on a pogo stick – she'll need the pogo stick to do this.
- A company asks members of the public to dress up as vampires and meet at a London location to promote their film – each person gets a DVD of the film for free.
- A business tries to give away more product samples in an hour than any other by hitting the streets and handing them out like crazy.
- A TV show asks people to donate products so they can build a giant art project for a gallery.
- A member of the public trying to run a marathon asks for costume manufacturers to send him a silly costume.
- A video game enthusiast wants to set the record for most hours playing a game – he then gets sponsored by an energy drink company that provides him with drinks, the game, a console and a TV.
- A hypnotist wants to try and lure the largest group of people into a trance – to get the people there, he offers free tickets to his show.
- A racing fan wants to break the record for most events visited in a year. He asks for a sponsor and is sent to hundreds of events for free, in return for wearing a branded tee-shirt at every one.
- A singer attempts to sing for the most hours in a row – she hopes this will get her a record contract at the end, by raising awareness of her talents.

chapter 9

Choose Your Market

With 90 possible solutions and nine distinct avenues you could go down, you should now have a fairly good idea of what you can offer a company. Even if you haven't quite got there yet, let the above ideas sit in your mind while you read the next section and something will come to you.

We're now going to move on to a different category and talk about the types of companies you could contact, the advantages and disadvantages of each, and some general tips for initiating contact.

Keep your unique offer in the back of your mind, as it's possible to twist offers in different ways for different companies. And remember that, although not all companies are right for every offer, you can certainly try more than one approach per company.

PR Agencies

We touched a little bit on PR agencies in the earlier section on choosing the right person to contact, and this is because PR agencies don't fit into the typical boxes of marketing and sales that you'll find in other companies. They have a different type of contact and need a different approach.

The good news is that, hands down, PR agencies are the best source for free products. Of all the free products I have received, 70% have come direct from PR agencies and there's a very simple reason for this: PR agencies represent more than one company.

So while contacting a company will give you access to their entire product range, a PR company can give you access to the product ranges of multiple companies. What's more, if you can convince a PR company that your unique offer is strong, they are more likely to send you products from more than one company.

As a comparison, if you approach a company directly they may send you something free originally, but then you'll have to wait a short while before contacting them again. Otherwise you'll offend them by attempting to take up too much of their time.

The other benefit of PR agencies is that they are the most receptive group to new ideas. Their employees are hired purely to promote the products they represent. This is done by sending out press releases and encouraging people to try certain products. While press releases may be written up in different publications, there's nothing more powerful than giving people the chance to actually get their hands on something.

In terms of how PR agencies go about this, they can be as inventive as they like, and many are given free rein to promote a product so long as they stick to a budget. There will be a set number of samples for each product, and it will be role of the PR company to get as much publicity as possible using this.

So kudos to the PR people who are very keen to try and find original ways to get these products out there. Sure, they could just send a product to each major news source and stick their feet up, but there are lots of PR companies out there who have an ear to the ground for unique promotional opportunities. And what's more unique than our unique offers?

There is but one thing to look out for with PR agencies and that's simply those agencies who insist on everything being returned. This happens most with major electronic and clothing brands, and although I've received free products from both, there have been occasions when I've been asked to give a product back.

This happens mostly when a PR agency has a very limited number of products, or has been told by the company they represent that everything must be returned. It doesn't matter if you're the top-selling magazine, or an average Joe looking for a freebie, if a product is marked that it must be returned then there's not a lot you can do to fight it.

To handle this dilemma, you need to make it clear from the first contact that you are only looking for free products and will not return those sent. This may make you seem like a bit of a scrounger, but it is the truth, and if you aren't up front about this you'll only get emails later asking you to return the product.

For some of my earlier attempts at getting free stuff I made no mention of this fact, for fear that admitting my true reason for wanting the product would make me seem cheap and an unreliable form of product exposure for the PR agency. This changed the first time I was asked to give a product back. I realised I had no leg to stand on, especially from a legal standpoint, so I had to buckle to the pressure.

I've come back to this one a few times, but it's worth remembering we are not trying to be liars, thieves or con artists. We want to work together with companies to expose their products and to build long working relationships that give them the confidence to send us something time and time again. We certainly don't want some renegade running around, tricking companies into sending them stuff and then running off into the sunset.

In addition, you shouldn't underestimate the potential for companies to misread your emails. After the incident sending the product back, I changed all my emails to state "We will review any product I am sent for free" and in time this led me to realise that this could be misinterpreted as me writing about products without charging a fee.

So I updated my emails again, this time clearly stating that, "We offer to review any product for free to over 30,000 visitors, our only rule being that we can keep the product when we're finished."

The above example is straight to the point, so makes it exactly clear. Since sending this email I have maintained the same success rate, and have yet to be asked to return a product. In fact, of all the products I've received for free, I've only ever had to return two, so generally there is a very good understanding among PR agencies that once they send you a product it is yours to keep.

The third factor to consider with PR agencies is that a lot of them contain genuinely nice people who are more than happy to hear from you. Of all the companies I have called, the people within PR agencies are the nicest around. Back when I was trying to get my first free products (and hadn't even invented the "persona" or "unique offer") I spoke to a PR agency and was amazed by just how much time they had for me. I'd just about scraped a website together to talk about products and it had maybe five or six articles, yet the PR person was kind enough to give me a chance and send me something for free.

Now she's one of my best contacts within the industry and the products she has sent have been seen in photo shoots in newspapers around the world as a result. Because she was so helpful in the early days, if I can hold one of her products in a photo shoot, I will. It's my way of returning her help when I was starting out.

I won't name her here for fear everyone who reads this will pounce on her and try to get freebies, but needless to say I have met plenty of other nice people at PR companies, who I'm sure will have the same patience for many of you.

If you've decided PR agencies are for you, then make sure you know exactly whom you want to speak to before you first make contact. If you send an unlabelled email to them without a named contact it will get deleted.

Likewise, if you ring a PR agency and don't know whom you want then you'll just speak to a receptionist or could end up speaking to anyone within the agency (who may not have products to send out, or even have a product that fits with your offer).

Therefore we'd better make sure we discover the best person for the call. Surprisingly, it's very hard to find PR contacts on a PR agency website, so your best bet is to look in the press areas of large companies, as this is where PR contacts are often listed.

Not every large company will have a PR agency, and some will have one in house, but those that do more often than not will list those details on their website. After all, if you spend all that money recruiting an agency – so you don't have to deal with calls from the press – then you'd better make sure everyone can find those details easily.

If worst comes to worst and you really want a certain product but can't find any distinct contact details, then knowing the PR agency who represents them can give you a decent head start. Likewise, if you visit a PR company website and can see that on the client list they represent a brand you like, this can be enough of a starting point.

Should you find yourself in this situation, you will need to ring the PR company directly and ask who is responsible for the PR for that brand. Email won't work in this scenario but a phone call is generally enough to find you the details you need, or for you to get transferred to the right person.

If you are heading down this road, just bear in mind that many of the largest companies have different agencies for their various brands. So you may see a brand on a PR website, but they could represent a different product from that manufacturer than the one you want. If you want an MP3 player from a company that also makes missile defence systems, for example, just be sure you're contacting the right person for the product you want.

Big Companies

Just because PR companies have the maximum potential for returns, that doesn't mean that by definition you should use them as the only source. Big companies (i.e. those with multiple stores and lots of products) can be very fruitful if you get them on your good side.

There are many companies who simply don't have PR agencies. So unless you want to rule them out completely, you'll need to understand the best way to approach them.

Thankfully, big companies are very similar to PR agencies in terms of their structure and potential for handing out products. In fact, a lot of larger companies do their own PR in house, and so have the same sort of mission statement as PR agencies: Promote the product and get people talking about it.

If a company does have a PR agency in house they are likely to at least listen to your ideas and want to work with you. The downside is that big companies can carry a lot more bureaucratic headaches, and of all the company types they are generally the slowest to send out any products.

For example: the PR contact may love your idea, but they could need sign-off from their manager, legal department and the product manager. These contacts will likely have many other responsibilities and therefore your request will fall down their list of priorities or be denied if it doesn't manage to appease everyone involved in the process.

You'll also encounter this issue if a company has a marketing or sales department that take up your request. It's frustrating, for sure, but not impossible, and often just requires a little bit of patience and calling up a few extra times to remind them you still exist.

As with PR agencies, you'll need to make it clear you can't return any products, although this seems to be less of an issue with large companies, as their supply of free products will be the biggest of all the company types. As an added bonus, they're the most aware of how much it costs to make the product, so if your offer is seen as contributing more value to the company than the cost of the product, then it's a far easier sell.

One thing large companies are often against is charities. If your unique offer includes any form of charity component, then it is likely to be refused. To see if this is likely to be the case, browse the company website to see if they already support any charities. If they do, it's unlikely they'll consider your offer as they have other charity activity and a lot of organisations will not associate with other charities in case it opens the door for more.

It's a cynical approach but one shared by many large companies, and there's very little you can do about it. Fantastic unique offer or not, if they already support a charity it reduces your chances drastically. Don't be deterred, however, as not all companies have charities they support, so there will be some who will choose to support you.

Even if your unique offer isn't charity related, it can be perceived as charitable. Some of the first rejections I received were from large companies who told me they don't send freebies to charities. This was despite my initial letters mentioning nothing to do with charities. The problem was that my letters came across as someone begging, and simply didn't make an impact in the short time they were read by each company.

I've resolved this since by ensuring anything I send a large company is brief and to the point. I stress the unique offer very early on, and state clearly how this will benefit them. I then word the letter to read more along the lines of, "I will do this if you send me a product" than, "Send me a product and I will do this." It's a subtle difference, but one which changes the reader's perception instantly.

If you get rejected you can turn the size of the company against it, to give you multiple attempts. Marketing turned you down? Then write a letter to sales asking them the same thing. If they turn you down, then give customer support a ring. Explain what you've been trying to do and that no one will listen to you about it. If that doesn't work you can always come up with a new offer and repeat the process from the start.

If you understand rules like this, you'll soon see how the size of a big company can both work for you and against it. You'll still encounter people who only want to send products to big established journalists, but likewise you will discover those who want exposure for their brand which their competition do not have, and this is where you come in.

Little Companies

By the very nature of their size, little companies have the least to give of all the potential sources. A further negative is that they are much more aware of what it will cost them to give you a product for free, and they're the most keen to see results if they do. For them, losing a product with no gain affects the very same profits that go into their pocket at night.

This doesn't mean you should write little companies off altogether. For one, they're the quickest source to approve requests and send out products. I've called little companies towards the end of the working day and then received something in the post the very next day. That's rare with PR agencies and unheard of with large companies, and it's purely because there's no approval needed. If they want to send you something then they'll pack it up and go ahead.

If you can find someone who is passionate about their product and not getting the exposure they need in the usual places, then your unique offer can be quite powerful. What's more, if the company is in your local area you may be just what they're looking for. If your offer is to try their product then you may buy more in the future and provide them with valuable feedback. Likewise, if your offer is exposing the product, you could be just the kind of word-of-mouth marketing they need.

So with both these points in mind, it's important to weigh up the possibilities. If your unique offer is using your day job and you also work for a local business then there are fantastic possibilities to be had, especially in terms of bartering. If you can offer them one of your products or services in return, then your two local businesses will be working together. This could build a bridge between the two companies that creates a long-standing professional relationship.

It's unlikely a large company would ever barter with another company, so for those going down the job unique offer route, little companies are your best bet.

When contacting little companies it's far harder to pin down a specific contact. It may be the company only has a few employees and that a marketing or sales contact simply doesn't exist. So the usual rules of looking for these departments go out of the window, and you may instead find a company where everyone does a bit of everything.

There's every possibility that the company's website will give away no contact details forcing you to make the hardest of all contact methods – a cold call. If this occurs, all you can really do is try and gather as much information about the company before you call. That way, you can at least act like you have done some research when the company asks questions of you.

If you aren't confident on the phone then this is not the best option, and while an email is a possibility most small businesses will be too busy to respond or take your offer seriously. Despite all this, should you fancy a challenge, or simply want to work with some local businesses, it is very possible to get free stuff this way.

Retail

Contrary to popular belief, walking into a shop and asking to be given something for nothing is not the best method of getting freebies. It is by far the hardest method you'll ever try and therefore should only be attempted by those who have spent months refining their persona and technique.

Why is it so difficult? Well, for one it's completely face to face, meaning only those who are very confident and able to think on their feet will be able to succeed. Unlike other contact methods, you can't duck away and think of a second response.

Second, it's very unlikely that the person you need to speak to will be able to talk to you at the time you arrive. An added headache is that the marketing or sales contacts may be located in a different building or work on a different day – in which case you've wasted a trip.

It's not like you can just turn up and convince any sales assistant to give you something. For one, they simply don't have the authority to do so, and two, if they took the initiative and did give you something, they'd probably get fired.

Option three is that they ask their manager, who probably has little power for giving away freebies. Push the issue too much and you could be escorted out by security.

So wouldn't you rather stay at home making phone calls and emails? I thought so.

If you are still convinced this method is for you, there are a few steps you can take to increase your chances:

1. *Book ahead*: Don't fall into the trap that the one way to deal with retail stores is in person. Check the website for the store and try to find their number. Then call ahead and ask who is in charge of PR or

marketing. On this occasion it's best not to ask for sales, as technically everyone in the store is in charge of this.

You'll probably then discover the person you need to speak to works in another place, so get those details and make contact via letters, phone or email. If the person you need to speak to does work in the store then try to speak to them over the phone, or ask to arrange a meeting.

2. *Bring a camera crew*: It doesn't matter if you have a professional film crew behind you, or a mate with their video camera, walking into a store with someone behind you holding a camera is a nice trick. If you've chosen a unique offer involving video this is even better, as it will reinforce what you are proposing.

    If that isn't your strategy, it really doesn't matter. The point is that walking into a retail store with a camera is going to get you noticed. It may get you escorted-out-of-the-building noticed, or it may be just the thing to encourage the store manager to listen to what you have to say.

3. *Make the most of face to face*: If someone has agreed to meet with you, you'll probably have 15-30 minutes of their time. None of the other sources of free products will give you anywhere near as much time, so make the most of it. You should still present your offer up front (to grab their attention) and then use the extra time to talk more about what you have to offer and what you have got for free to date. As before, if you're a beginner you won't be able to do a lot of this, so that's another reason to save it for when you have some freebies under your belt.

If you can master this source then you truly will be a king among freebie-seekers. If not, then there are plenty of other ways, or the easier option of:

Trade Shows

If face-to-face conversations seem like your sort of thing then rather than retail I'd suggest trade shows as your first port of call. These shows are designed for companies to sell their products to other retail stores, so for us even to be there is a little bit naughty – but, nevertheless, if you want to spend an afternoon getting stuff for free, you won't find a much more successful place to do it than a trade show.

But first a quick distinction. There are shows companies put on that are for the public. They're often tied to a TV show or magazine and will charge you a fee to get in. As you enter you'll find the arena is full of people, and that talking to anyone on a stand is a nightmare. These are not the shows we will be attending.

Instead, the shows we will be going for are called "trade shows", and that's because they are supposed to only be for members of the trade, such as shops. This is quite frustrating as these shows have far less people and have the ideal marketing and sales contacts on the stand waiting to hear what you have to say. Oh, and the shows are free too.

So how can you gain access to these most secret of shows? The key is press access. If your unique offer includes talking about a product in any way, shape or form (blog, video, expert, group) then you are a journalist and gaining access is relatively simple.

Before we get to that, it's important to teach you how to find these shows, as they won't be advertised on TV or given much awareness to the public. Your best source is to find your local exhibition hall and to browse their website. Most of these sites list all upcoming shows and include links to their websites so you can register for tickets.

Shows will vary from those specific to a type of industry to seasonal shows that include a wide range of different products for the spring, summer and winter sales periods. Either way, if you can fit your unique offer to the type of product that will be shown, then go ahead and hunt down the ticket registration page.

There's no excuse for any of these shows charging for tickets, especially if you pre-register, so if they try to charge you then look elsewhere. The last thing we want to do is pay to attend a show when there are countless other free ones out there.

When it comes to registering for the show, list yourself as a journalist and request press access. This isn't technically a lie or breaking any laws, as you are planning on talking about products. If you can put together something you have written/filmed already, then that's even better and more likely to result in access too. It also makes your claim of being a journalist even more legitimate.

Once you've finished the registration it will be reviewed by the show and following acceptance you'll be sent your press pass. I've never been turned down for a single show, and am starting to wonder if forms are even checked – but on the off-chance you are rejected, simply try again for a different show.

Before the date of the show you'll also be sent a list of all the exhibitors. This is a gold mine, as the chances are you'll only be able to attend the show for a day, especially if you have a day job and can only attend the weekend portion of the show. Therefore you can use the exhibitors list to pre-plan your day and decide whom to see.

When working through the list, try to find companies that are of a decent size and who have PR departments. You can learn more about any company in attendance by searching for them online, and some trade shows will give an overview of each company on their website.

You can take this planning one step further and find out the best contact for each exhibitor online first. Better yet, if time is on your side you can contact the companies before the show, run through your offer and arrange to see them to explain more at the show itself. This gives you the benefit of walking on to each stand and knowing you will be seen to and that your offer will be taken seriously.

Hopefully the exhibitors list will open your mind to other companies you've never seen before. It's pointless to attend an exhibition hoping to get just one product from one company. Instead, you should take the day to talk through your offer with a wide range of companies and gain a number of contacts that can be approached later.

To this end it's important you don't underestimate the importance of business cards. To save you an expense, an online search for "free business cards" tends to return countless results for companies who will print you some for free (on the presumption you will buy more later) and you won't even need a unique offer to get them to do so.

On the cards include your name, address, phone number and email address. If you've used a website as part of your offer put that on there too, even if it's just the place you store your videos or photos. Don't use your business cards from work, unless you have a unique offer around your job, as this could come back to haunt you.

While at the show, hand out your business cards like they are candy, ensuring everyone you speak to gets one. After the shows a lot of people on the stands get calls from people they never spoke to, claiming all sort of lies, so by giving them your business card it ensures they can check if you spoke to them before or not.

In addition, giving someone a business card is a fantastic excuse for you to take one of theirs. Even if a conversation ends badly, giving someone a business card instinctively makes them want to give you one back. You then have their details, which tend to be direct contact numbers and email addresses, allowing you to follow up after the show.

Let's run through a typical exchange:

- You walk on to the stand and get someone's attention.
- They spot your name badge and that you are a journalist. They ask what you do.
- You explain your offer briefly and that you'd like to speak to someone in marketing or sales.
- They tell you no one who does that is on the stand.
- You ask for the contact details of someone who does.
- If they have it, they give you a business card, or write their details down on a piece of paper. If not, they give you the main office number.
- You walk away, noting down the name of the person who helped you.

In this scenario you have gained some information, and although no specific conversation has been had, you can now contact the person for marketing or the main office. Noting down the name of the person you spoke to is essential as it means one of two things:

1. When you do contact the marketing person, you can say who gave you their details.

2.   After the show you can call them and ask for the marketing details if they didn't have them first time around.

How would that exchange look if we were able to speak to the marketing contact?

- You walk on to the stand and get someone's attention.
- They spot your name badge and that you are a journalist. They ask what you do.
- You explain your offer briefly and that you'd like to speak to someone in marketing or sales.
- They go to fetch the right person.
- You are faced with the marketing manager. He asks you what you do.
- You explain your offer (assuming the previous person didn't say anything).
- The marketing manager considers the offer and either gives you their details for a follow-up or says no.

If they say no, that's OK. Better to move on to another stand than harass one person until they give in. A lot of people will pass each stand, so you have pretty much a one-shot chance of impressing each person. Generally this works in your favour, as if your offer makes them even a little curious they will give you their details.

What won't happen is that they'll go off to a back room, grab a bunch of free samples and then give them to you. They will want to consider your offer in depth after the show, and it's unlikely they will have enough faith in you after one minute to let you walk away with something.

That's not to say no one ever walks away from trade shows with anything. I've seen people attend with suitcases and walk out with them bulging with products. Sadly for us, these people are store managers, and they are given these products because they already buy a lot of products from the trade companies.

However, journalists need not leave a trade show empty-handed, as you have something that the store managers do not: a press badge. Most trade shows will have a press room, and this should be the first place you visit on arrival at the exhibition. This room will be a fixed location that is in the same place for every exhibition in that arena, and anyone who works at the exhibition centre will be able to tell you where it is.

The press room will be blocked off so you will need to present your press badge for entry. Thankfully, there are so many random magazines with different names that you needn't work for a major paper to get access, and so whatever nickname you have chosen for your unique offer or persona should be fine to get you access. On one occasion I was asked to present my ID as well, so be sure to use your real name on all the documents.

Inside the press area are three things you'll want to grab:

1. *Press Releases*: These will give you the PR contacts for many of the brands at the show and a rough guide to their products. After the show you can use these details to make contact and build your list of press contacts who send free stuff.

2. *Product Samples*: Oh yes. The press room will almost always contain samples of products at the show. This is why you'll need to go to this room first of all, as once they're gone, that's it (and believe me when I say everyone else will be wanting these samples). I've attended trade shows before where I've hit the press room, then walked back to my car to unload three bags of free stuff, and then gained more samples in the afternoon. Every product got exposure from me after the show, so I didn't just take the products without giving something back.

3. *Show Guide*: This is an expanded version of the exhibitors list and the information on the trade show website. It's a who's who guide that details everyone there and gives you hundreds of contact details to use after the show ends. You can buy these guides outside of the press room for anywhere between £10 and £100, but they are sometimes available for free in the press area. Well worth grabbing.

As you can probably tell by the fact I've written so much on this one source, trade shows work. If nothing else you'll come away with countless new people to contact and relationships that can be nurtured over time. Compared to walking into a retail store, visiting a trade show is countless times more valuable in the long run.

chapter 10

Types of Contact Methods

Feeling confident? Good, because we're about to make contact with our first company. Before we do you'll have to decide which contact method you want to use. Your choices are:

- Letters
- Email
- Phone
- Face to Face
- Social Networks

If you've got your heart set on one, then jump to that section and read how to do it. If not, then check out all five of the sections below and take your pick. I'm not going to teach you what an email or letter is, but I will show you how to maximise your usage of each approach so you get the most out of it.

Don't forget to read the final few chapters, which give some added tips on what to do after you make contact.

Contact Methods – Letters

Just because a lot of the tips in this book are for online tools doesn't mean the traditional letter is completely useless in contacting companies. With so many people using emails as a means of contact, letters are becoming more effective because they are the rarer format and therefore get people's attention.

Think how many emails you get every day compared to letters. I'll bet you open pretty much every letter, and if it's from someone new you'll at least skim the content. With email, you've probably deleted all the new emails within a matter of minutes, without getting much further than the subject line.

That's not to say with a letter there's any excuse for rambling on. You'll still need to write something concise, but this is the format that has the most chance of being read. In addition, if you do grab someone's attention you can provide a bit more information than an email, as a page of A4 in the form of a letter is much more appealing than a really long email.

So, taking into consideration the strengths of the format, let's look at the potential content we can include:

Intro – addressed to a named person in the company
Paragraph One – what is your offer?
Paragraph Two – why you chose the company
Paragraph Three – why should they pick you?
Paragraph Four – next steps
Paragraph Five – summary

All in all, that should end up as less than a sheet of A4 (including all the address information at the top). I'm not going to teach you how to format your address, but here's an example of how those paragraphs could look:

■ *Intro* – addressed to a named person in the company
  Dear Mr. Smith,

■ *Paragraph One* – what is your offer?
If you are looking for a place to promote your product in the next few months may I suggest **BloominGoodReviews.co.uk**? We are a group of **writers** who **review any product that we are sent**. There's no cost to you, and all we ask is that we can keep any product we're sent.

■ *Paragraph Two* – why you chose the company
We would like to review a product from **Company X** as this will fit in well with our other **reviews of books** and you appear to be one of the **market leaders at the moment**. We are especially interested in the **Company X X1200** but are happy to review any product you may have.

■ *Paragraph Three* – why should they pick you?
Over the last three months we have reviewed **20 different products** in your sector, **attracting 1,000 visitors** and numerous positive comments.

■ *Paragraph Four* – next steps
For more information, please contact **Mike Essex** on the details at the bottom of this email. On receipt of your product we will aim to have a **review** live within a week.

■ *Paragraph Five* – summary
Thank you for taking the time to read this letter. If you have any questions we will be more than happy to help.

That's one example, and the items in bold text can easily be changed to suit a different unique offer. Let's look at an alternate possibility:

■ *Intro* – addressed to a named person in the company
Dear Mrs. Jones,

■ *Paragraph One* – what is your offer?
If you are looking for a place to promote your product in the next few months may I suggest our **video marketing services**? We are a group of **film makers who film unique videos for any products**. There's no cost to you, and all we ask is that we can keep any product we're sent.

■ *Paragraph Two* – why you chose the company
We would like to review a product from **Wakeup Energy Drinks** as this will fit in well with our other **videos** and you appear to be one of the **most interesting and fun loving brands**. We are especially interested in the **Wakeup Juicy Fruits Drink**, but are happy to film any product you may have.

■ *Paragraph Three* – why should they pick you?
Over the last three months we have **videoed 10 different drinks** in your sector, **attracting lots of online views** and numerous positive comments.

■ *Paragraph Four* – next steps
For more information please contact **Dave Jones** on the details at the bottom of this email. On receipt of your product we will aim to have a **video** live within a week.

■ *Paragraph Five* – summary
Thank you for taking the time to read this letter. If you have any questions we will be more than happy to help.

Fairly simple really. Ideally, you should tweak a little more than the bold elements, as the last thing you want is for someone else to read this and send the exact same email, but in terms of the approach it should get you started

Contact Methods – Emails

While emails don't have quite the same visibility as letters, I personally prefer them as a contact method. It's very easy to craft one email for an industry, pull all the contacts together and send off multiple emails in one go. All you need to do is change the name and company reference, add the email address and hit send.

This scattergun approach is ideal as it gives you the best chance of ensuring returns quickly. It's no substitute for taking the time to research each company at length and writing unique emails, but in the early stages it's better to use a one-size-fits-all email and try to cover a wide portion of the manufacturers in one go.

Like the trade show our goal is to get people's attention so we can follow up with further information, and then show how much we've researched about the company. This research can be completed on receipt of the second email and before sending your reply, so you don't have to spend hours finding every little detail on a company if all they do is hit delete.

Email keeps many of the advantages of mail, such as the ability to hide behind the computer and include a decent-sized chunk of information. This is slightly less than with a letter, so we'll need to be a little quicker. We'll also need to have a very catchy subject line that encourages people to open the email, but which doesn't make us seem like spammers.

As with letters we can use a similar, but shorter structure:

Intro – addressed to a named person in the company
Paragraph One – what is your offer and why should they pick you?
Paragraph Two – why you chose the company
Paragraph Three – next steps

So we've merged two paragraphs and dropped the summary. Here's an example:

Subject: Give Back Your Unwanted Product Samples

■ *Intro* – addressed to a named person in the company
Hi John,

■ *Paragraph One* – what is your offer and why should they pick you?
We're up to something at Mike Essex.co.uk. In short, we're asking everyone in the world of PR and marketing to donate their unwanted product/press samples to a charity auction. As an added bonus, each product will be discussed on the www.mikeessex.co.uk website as well.

■ *Paragraph Two* – why you chose the company
This can be a brand new product or discontinued stock, the idea being simply that money has been generated for charity from thin

air: "blags to riches", as we are calling it. We have chosen your agency as you have a fantastic list of clients we would like to work with on this project.

■ *Paragraph Three* – next steps
For more information drop me an email on mike@blagman.co.uk, visit http://www.mikeessex.co.uk/2008/12/blagback-donating-unwanted-press.html, or pop your samples in the post to: [Address]

"Next steps" needs to include your postal address, as this won't be on the email by default. You should also include phone and email contact details. In addition I've included a link to a web page that explains the topic more, making up for the lack of space in the email.

This is actually a real email I used to get products for a charity auction. So let's write a different example, this time for someone using their friends to promote a product.

Subject: Cheese-Eating Contest – Samples Needed

■ *Intro* – addressed to a named person in the company
Hello John, my fellow cheese lover!

■ *Paragraph One* – what is your offer and why should they pick you?
I have been a long time buyer of Chummy Cheese, and you know what, I feel like a change. Ever since my friends and I held a bet to see who could eat the most, I've wanted to sample more cheeses from around the world.

■ *Paragraph Two* – why you chose the company
As such, I'm looking to jump ship to a new brand, and after searching online I came across your website. Looking at the cheeses on offer, I'd really like to introduce the guys to a new taste sensation.

■ *Paragraph Three* – next steps
To help me do so, would you be willing to send me some samples of your cheese? I'll make sure to include it in the next cheese-eating contest, which is sent to 100 friends online. You can view more on our contest at [Facebook page link].

Name
Phone/Email/Address

There's a certain cheekiness to this that would only work in email format, but you can be very serious or light-hearted. It all comes back to your persona and the type of image you want to portray. Once the email is written, change a few details and send it on again.

Whatever you do, don't copy all the email addresses into the "to" or "cc" fields and send the same email to everyone. They won't appreciate seeing each other's names in the email, and it really will work against you.

Contact Methods – Telephone

Unlike the above methods, calling a company is a far more unpredictable scenario. For starters, you have to make sure you're speaking to someone who can actually help. Assuming the research earlier was top notch (and the company website had the right details), this should be as simple as asking for the right person.

However, there are numerous different types of personalities you will encounter when making a phone call, and this means a simple request to speak to someone can be met with a wall of questions. Depending on the type of person, this can be easy or an absolute nightmare, and it means writing an example phone call isn't possible.

So instead I offer you this breakdown on the types of people you will encounter on the phone, and the best ways to deal with them.

Wise One

Most professional companies will have a "wise one" on their main reception, especially those where there is one main number for all employees. I have given them this name because they are used to people ringing up trying to sell products, so they are wise to the type of methods people use to sneakily speak to people without a planned call.

They will ask you questions to confirm that you know the name of someone in the department and that they are expecting your call. If you did your research earlier you will be aware of the contact name so that shouldn't be a problem. In terms of having a planned call you can't really lie for this one. Best just to say "No" and that you are a customer who has a good marketing idea for the brand.

If they refuse to put you through, then ask for an email address so you can at least detail what you would like to offer. This is typically given out, and if not you can return to your earlier contact list, send an email to the main company email address, and mark it for their attention.

Blocker

A "blocker" is similar to a "wise one", but even more sceptical. They tend to be secretaries for specific people. Their role will be to allow through only the most important calls, and to turn everything else down.

Unless they have spoken to you before, you've very little chance of getting through. So instead detail your unique offer to them and ask if there is anyone else in the company you could speak to. As the secretary they should at least note down the request, and if someone else does exist that can help they'll hopefully have enough company knowledge to point you in the right direction.

Newbie

Some companies will put their most junior employee on the central reception: a really frustrating experience for us, as we want someone who knows the company inside out. Most requests for specific contact names will result in a confused noise and you being put on hold while they ask someone else to help.

However, this naivety can be used to your advantage. If you are calling a company, and don't know a named contact, a newbie is the most likely type of person to forward you on without even asking why you are calling.

Waster

While a "newbie" lacks knowledge but is ultimately helpful, a "waster" is their unhelpful brother or sister. They still lack knowledge, but are no help at all when it comes to putting you in touch with the right person. They'll speak forever, and rattle off ridiculous conversational topics that bear no relation to the call.

You could spend the time telling them your offer, but they are the type of people who will not even write it down, and will listen to you more because they are bored than through any desire to help. If you find this type of contact, strike them from your list and ask if anyone in another department can help.

Now you know what to look for, it should be easy to spot which type of contact you are dealing with. This leaves out the really cooperative people who care what you have to say, but there's no need to classify them in negative boxes like the ones above. If you find a prospect who is keen on your offer it will become apparent through the conversation, and the way they are asking positive questions.

In short, your goal is to achieve the following type of conversation:

1. Ask for your contact, or the marketing/PR department.

2. Make (very) small talk asking how they are/how the product is doing.

3. Explain your offer as briefly and succinctly as possible. This should include the core benefit and leave other parts open for you to explain once you have their attention.

4. Give contact details and take a direct line/email if you don't already have one.

5. Follow up with a full email outlining the benefits of your offer soon after the call.

Given that we've got to follow up with an email anyway, you may ask why we didn't just do that in the first place. Well, because we've already made contact our email has a far greater chance of being read and actioned than something out of the blue.

Once you gain confidence in your abilities you will ideally want to call every contact before sending them an email and to reach people in this way. Alternatively, you'll find contacts first from trade shows or scanning websites, and then speak to them by phone first as well. If you keep trying to reach someone on the phone and they never answer, you can try a letter to get their attention. Coupling all these ideas together makes your overall offering stronger.

The Persona Aspect

Talking on the phone is one of the biggest tests of your persona, because you simply cannot trick the conversation. You can't take the time to think and form a second reply, like you can with email or post.

Therefore, there are a few additional things to consider when talking on the phone that you should add to your persona. The first is that you shouldn't act like you've known the person all your life. Starting a conversation asking how things are is OK, but delving in to long conversations about a person's day-to-day life is weird for a first call.

Similarly don't start using casual conversational elements such as calling someone "mate" or "buddy". It may slip out from time to time, which is OK, but a long conversation with lots of references to the terms can put people off.

Then you'll need to make sure you don't mimic the contact's personality traits back to them. Remember your persona, and even if the contact is rude and has a strong accent, try not to be rude back or let their accent affect your own. This becomes easier with practice, and each time you let your guard down in this way, make a mental note not to let it happen again.

Other than that, I'd just advise you to not take it too seriously. If someone is offensive or refuses your offer, then thank them for their time and move on. Some people can be complete jerks on the phone, and that's just the pot luck of calling people at random. Remember that you aren't a salesperson and that you are trying to help them improve their brand or sales.

Do this and they will see your offer is genuine and at least worth a few minutes of their time.

Contact Methods – Face to Face

Back in the retail and trade show chapters, I revealed that face-to-face conversations are the hardest way to get free products. So I touched on ways to make this a little easier by planning scheduled appointments and ensuring an effective plan for the day. These are all good factors that improve the chances of success.

So instead of repeating those rules, let's instead take a look at some of the dynamics of getting freebies face to face.

The clear advantage is that face to face is a visual format. So if you want to show a demo video or photo for those projects, you can. If you've done anything similar to your offer before, take in a sample and try to prove that what you are offering is possible. If you have nothing to show, then try putting together a presentation to show ways other people have done similar things that were effective.

There's no need to take an entire suitcase of things with you, so this is really all about time. If you have a long time slot booked then you'll have a chance to show more. If you've only got 15 minutes then one small prop is plenty to talk about.

The second advantage of the format is that you have more control than in any other method. Unless you really offend someone they will be with you for the booked time, so you'll be able to make all your key points. People are far less likely to end a face-to-face meeting than to delete an email or hang up a phone call.

So come into the face-to-face meetings with a clear list of what you want to cover. This will probably look something like:

- why you chose the company
- your offer
- why they should choose you
- next steps

This can be in your head, or actually written down as a formal agenda for the meeting. Agendas are a great way to ensure all the points are discussed. You can tick each one off as you go, and the contact is given an overview at the start of what you want to discuss.

The above list is quite short, and that's deliberate. Just because you have a meeting it doesn't give you a licence to talk about anything and everything. Whether the meeting is 15 minutes or an hour, be sure to keep everything to the point. We want the contact to feel at ease and not to come away feeling their time was wasted.

This carries the same sort of disclaimers as a phone call. Be sure to keep your persona in check and don't copy the traits of the contact. Don't be rude or act like you've known them all your life.

Face-to-face meetings are more effective with multiple people, so don't be afraid to bring a buddy and share any products you get with them. If your unique offer involved friends or a group then that's even better, as you already have people that can be invited to the meeting.

Not everyone needs to speak for the meeting to be deemed a success, but of all the people in attendance there should be one strong leader who discusses the four core points. Then other people can add insights or be given various titbits to talk about during the presentation.

Play to the format's strengths and there is certainly something to be gained from face-to-face meetings. Don't expect anything to be given to you straight after the meeting, but be sure to gather as many contact details as you can for follow-ups via email or phone soon afterwards.

Contact Methods – Social Networks

When we researched contacts towards the start of this guide, I asked you to write a comments column and add any additional information about each contact. This data really comes in to its own when contacting people through social networks, and just as this format can be a good unique offer, it can also connect you to influential people that can help find information.

The first thing you'll need to do is set up a profile on each of the sites where you've spotted a prospective contact. So if they're on LinkedIn, Twitter or Facebook then sign up as yourself and create a real profile. Add as many details as you can to encourage contacts to read more about you and check to see if any of your friends use the networks already. This will help flesh out your profile and make it seem more natural.

Then include on your profile details of your unique offer. The three sites above have ways for you to do this. By leaving extra profile boxes on Facebook and LinkedIn you can add this data, and for Twitter you can post periodic updates on what you have been up to and other products you've received.

This data should include a nice summary of the offer, and give an email contact method for more information. If you don't want to use your real email address then create a new one on any online email site and use it strictly for this purpose. Don't include address or phone numbers, as this type of information can be manipulated on social networks.

Once all of this is done you should take a week to let the profile grow naturally. It can look very suspicious if a new profile with no history makes contact with someone outside their social circle. The last thing we want to do is offend a prospective contact due to impatience, so instead we'll spend this time building up the profile.

We've already added some friends, so take the time to understand the social network by contacting them. Messages can be anything you want, but try not to let your guard down too much. Drunken images and offensive messages may not look so good if a contact decides to delve a little deeper into your profile.

If you can see them, it's worth exploring the profiles of your prospective contacts and seeing what they like to talk about. If there are any product launches they are talking about, or interesting things they've said, make a note of these. The goal is to learn the things they like, so we can use this data to our advantage later.

After a week, return to the profiles of your contacts and send them a request to connect with you. This may be called a friend request or an invite, depending on the network. In the invite include information on why you are contacting them. It's best at this stage not to scare them off, so just opt for something along the lines of:

"I'm looking to connect with people in the X industry."

Replace X with the industry the contact works in and you're done. If they try to learn more about you first, your profile should help prove that you are indeed interested in that industry.

If they accept your invitation, you've then gained their attention in a very neutral way, making them more prone to listen to what you say in the future.

All of the three above networks make it so once you are connected you'll see everything the contact says and vice versa. This allows us to sow the seeds for our unique offer and encourage the contact to ask for more details.

Test this out by writing an update which reads:

"I'm looking for X to help me complete something special. Can anyone help?"

Replace X with the product you want, and you've dropped a major hint for the contact to find later. Follow this up with further posts developing the point and adding more details about the offer. Drop some other comments in between these posts, such as messages to friends or random things like thoughts on TV shows to make things continue to look natural. If you spotted anything the contact likes earlier, then allude to this.

During this time you should also be periodically reading the updates of your contact to see if they say anything of interest. If any of their posts reflect something you know about then get involved and send them a message back. This can be business-related, offer-related or even just a silly personal thing, such as their love for tea over coffee. If it resonates with you, then let them know it.

If you don't receive a response after another week and the hints go unnoticed, then send a message directly to the contact. This time you can give an overview of the offer and should presume that they have not read any of your comments. So include the basic details and leave some elements for them to be sent on a second contact (the next chapter).

Build up the relationship this way, and over time you can catch the eye of major contacts within different sectors. Often some of the busiest marketing professionals (who would be unreachable through their secretaries on the phone) devote a lot of time to social networks, and are far more responsive.

Another trick is to add people to your social network even if you've chosen to contact them by a different method. This shouldn't be done on the same day as your other message, as we're not trying to stalk the person. Leave it a few days and then add them.

Social networks are the last key to finding the right people and getting on their radar. They are a good backup to all the other contact methods, and are the best way to ensure you remain relevant even after getting something for free from someone.

chapter 11

Second Contact

The first contact you have with a company is by far the hardest – although it doesn't end there. There are a few possible scenarios that may play out next, and here are the best ways to approach them.

How Long Should I Wait for a Reply?

While you may be buzzing with excitement following your first contact, it's not uncommon to be disappointed if you don't get a reply within the hour. I used to spend most of the day refreshing my email, hoping for some sort of feedback.

If you've sent someone an email you can typically expect a reply within three days. After this time you've probably been filed away or deleted. Watch for out-of-office auto-replies when you send your message originally, or for any delivery messages that indicate the message may have been delayed. Then factor these into the time you wait.

For phone, if you can speak to the person you need to first time around, it's a win-win situation. If they don't answer and you've left a message you could be waiting up to a week for a reply. Three days is still the sensible waiting time, but the person may be in a string of meetings, or simply never check their voicemail. They could also be on holiday, and people are much worse at remembering to tell others they are away on voicemail than on email.

Letters are the slowest contact method, taking up to 28 days for a reply – a bit of a pain, but that's the frustration of the format, sadly.

For face to face, you'll get an instant reply and be given a phone number for a follow-up call. Again, leave three days after the conversation ends and then follow up.

If you've contacted someone through social media you should expect a reply within 24 hours. It's the fastest method, but bear in mind how often they update their status, as they may not even be using their account any more.

What If I Don't Get a Reply?

If you have waited patiently for the above time periods and still received nothing, it's worth doing the following:

Email: Send a second email to the same person with your original email below it. Add a small line of text at the top explaining that you are following up this email and are happy to discuss it over the phone if they'd prefer. If there is no reply after a week, try calling the person or writing them a letter.

Phone: Although you could wait a week to try again, it's OK to try another call every 2-3 days. Only leave a voicemail the first two times, and if you get nowhere after a few tries call reception, ask for the person's email, and try getting in touch that way.

Letter: If you've waited the fun-filled 28 days, don't bother sending another letter, and instead call the person and ask if they received your letter.

Face to Face: Keep trying the follow-up phone number every 2-3 days and follow the same steps as with the phone strategy.

Social Networks: Post another message on a completely different topic. If no reply after that, see if they have any profiles on other websites, or send them an email.

If after trying these methods you still get nowhere, it's best to leave it a month and repeat from the start with a new unique offer. Or simply find a more responsive company instead.

What If the Contact Details Are Wrong?

Just because someone's contact details are on a website doesn't make them true. I once rang a major teddy bear manufacturer to find that the PR agency on their website hadn't handled their account for two years.

It's a shame to go through research just to get an "email not found" or an awkward phone call with someone that doesn't know who you're talking about. Still, if this happens there's always the fallback of asking to speak to someone in marketing or sales. Most places are at least clued-in enough that they'll pass you on to a replacement person or forward a letter on accordingly, so your time hasn't always been wasted.

If you'd prefer not to make a phone call, then return to the website and try to find someone else in a similar job role, or even just email the receptionist and ask for details.

What If I Get Rejected?

With so many busy companies, or those who are just powerless/stuck in their ways, you will receive rejections. The aim is to go in broad with your product choices, so that rather than being turned down from one product, you have a higher chance of receiving it from one of a group of manufacturers.

Should you receive an email that rejects you, it's worth reading it with an open mind. Perhaps there is a problem with your offer, or the company will consider you in the future if you can fulfil certain criteria. Keep a word document of all the feedback you get, and try to look for patterns that may indicate future opportunities.

There's no one better to tell you what companies want than the companies themselves. This type of research is vital, and it's only through months of rejections I was able to create the unique offer. Hopefully I've saved you a lot of these rejections by putting down the process in this book, but I've no doubt there will be ways you can improve your offer over time.

Sometimes companies will fundamentally misunderstand your offer, and that's always a shame. It is worth contacting them again just to clarify any negative points they may have, as you can sometimes turn rejections in your favour. Just be sure not to turn into a sore loser. If they won't send you products because they expect something you can't deliver, then there's no point getting into an argument.

I Got a Positive Reply. Now What?

When someone does reply expressing interest in your offer, it could be as short as an email saying "Tell me more", or a huge checklist of criteria to fulfil.

Whatever the response, be sure to read it a couple of times and really digest what they need from you. Chop their reply into parts and look for the individual questions. If you're on the phone, don't be afraid to tell them you'll answer a particular question via email, if you don't have the answer to hand. Much better to do that than make up something you can't deliver.

No matter the format, don't feel like you have to reply instantly. For emails, letters and social networks, take the time to write something smart and read it back multiple times. On the phone, pauses are fine between answers, and be sure to give them enough time to speak.

With your reply, reiterate that you can't return any products. Then you've made it absolutely clear and it reduces the risk of anyone asking for returns. If they aren't OK with this, explain that to really test the product you'll need to try it in a way that wouldn't make it possible to return it. Taking the trainers example from earlier, we could say that we would use them in muddy conditions, so they wouldn't want them back.

Have I Left It Too Long to Reply?

Just as we may get frustrated if a company doesn't reply, they will do the same if you don't respond in a timely fashion. The rules for this are a little tighter than those we've given the companies (as we want to seem efficient), but here's what you should aim for:

Email: A same day response. If you're at work, this won't be during the company working day (as you probably won't read the email until 6-7), but if you email them back before you go to bed, that's fine. If it's a weekend, any time before the end of the weekend will suffice. If you've got a crazy day and can't reply, then stick an out-of-office auto-reply on your email.

Letter: Aim for a week max, unless they have given you a specific deadline. Send the letter first class to save some time, and if the company is very keen consider having them sign for the letter on arrival, so you know it got there safely.

Phone/Face to Face: If you've promised to send details to someone after a phone call or meeting, try to do so the same day by midnight. Should this not seem possible, then raise this during the meeting and make it clear why it will take you longer to get the information together.

Social Network: The toughest of all channels for response time. People expect very quick responses. Try to pre-empt this by staying on the site for 10 minutes after your initial contact. If they don't reply within 10 minutes then you can leave and ensure you reply within 8 hours. Don't fall into the trap of checking this frequently during your day job. It's addictive, and likely to land you in trouble.

They Seemed Interested But Not Any More

The life of anyone in sales, marketing or PR can fluctuate from calm to insanely busy, often in the same hour. You may catch someone's attention in a quiet moment and then find grabbing another response from them a real struggle.

This is a little bit out of your hands, and I've found patience to be far more successful than badgering someone with email after email. Try to consider your own job role and the demands you have. Yes, you are offering them exposure for their products, or increased sales, but they may have a big problem to contend with, and bosses demanding they deal with that now.

In this situation, the more you push for a response, the worse it will make the situation for them, and the less cooperative they will feel. A simple reminder is fine. As with the suggestions for lack of reply, it's OK to drop someone a quick email, or message. Doing this day after day with increasingly demanding requests isn't OK, and will turn all that goodwill against you.

If you really aren't getting anywhere it's worth leaving it for a couple of weeks and making a fresh contact after that. You should still contact the same person, and have the same offer, but add something along the lines of, "I hope everything has calmed down after the busy period."

Is There a Time I Shouldn't Reply?

Always consider seasonality with the companies you contact. If you can reach someone during a quiet period, you've fantastically improved your chances of getting on their radar.

By seasonality, I'm referring to the changes in workload that come from the different time periods of the year. So don't contact anyone over major holidays like Christmas or Easter. You may have time on your hands while not at work, but the chances are your message will end up in a bulk delete on their first day back.

Likewise, if their product is likely to be really popular in a certain month, try to contact them a few months before this. That way you'll give them a chance to gain extra promotion for their key period, but they won't yet be swamped with the 101 things that need to be planned before that point.

So if they sell Christmas trees contact them in September. If they sell sunglasses aim for March. Not every company will have these key periods, but most will at least expect a sales rise at Christmas, unless their product is more useful when it's warm.

If they reply to you, these rules go out of the window, and you can reply normally.

chapter 12

Fulfil the Offer

As you've probably gathered by now, trust is a big part of this process, none more so than in the fulfilment of your unique offer. Sure, it's easy to take the freebie, cobble together something in a few minutes and claim that's the offer done, but our aim is to wow the company, encouraging them to return in the future.

In addition, the better job we do in this stage of the process the more appealing we will be able to make ourselves to other companies in the future. Imagine you've made the first company that sent you something for free really happy. In turn, they may provide you with a testimonial or recommend you to others.

You can then use this recommendation the next time you contact companies. As you detail the offer, you can drop in the companies you've satisfied in the past, and then some of their comments. This creates a vote of confidence for future companies, and legitimises your email, creating trust and improving the likelihood of them accepting your offer.

To simplify this, the diagram below shows the cyclical process involved. Each free product you get feeds into the next, building confidence with other companies.

Following this process, it's easy to see that a process of constant refinement is ideal, and we'll talk a little more about how to tweak your offer and persona in the next chapter.

For now, let's focus on how we can wow the company that has just sent us the product. Assuming that you've followed the earlier steps and were truthful when suggesting your offer, then you'll already have a vague idea that you will be able to fulfil your role.

While you may have decided you could fulfil the offer, there might be a few parts you're slightly unsure on. So before you get started, quickly break down your offer to make sure you have everything you need:

1. What do you need to fulfil the offer?
2. Which people do you need involved?
3. Where are you completing your offer?
4. How can you prove the offer has been completed?
5. How will you gather attention for the offer?

1 – What do you need to fulfil the offer?

A lot of the strategies for free stuff will require a physical item for their completion. For example, if you want products for an auction, then you'll need a table for the products. These items needn't cost money – just use your home, and your table – but the point is to ensure you have all the items needed before getting started.

Similarly, if you are taking photos or filming videos, then ensure you have the proper kit.

2 – Which people do you need involved?

Your unique offer may just involve you in a room drinking energy drinks, in which case you can skip this step. Other strategies may require the involvement of others such as any groups you start, or the "friend" style unique offers. If this is the case, now is the time to tell everyone that you've received the product and are about to fulfil the offer.

Draw up a list of all the people required to complete your offer and make sure everyone is briefed on what they need to do. This will depend on your offer, but it's better to give everyone a warning than suddenly to arrive and demand they help you.

3 – Where are you completing your offer?

This may be a physical location, or if you're using any the online strategies it will be through a blog, forum or video site. For online, if you haven't already then hop on to your site of choice and register a profile. Provide as much information for others to read as possible, as we want a lot of people to stumble upon your profile as you complete your offer.

If it's a physical location then ensure you can arrive there on the day you need in order to complete your offer. So if you've offered to mow the lawn of a business, make sure you can get there on the specific day you'd like.

4 – How can you prove the offer has been completed?

This is the most important step of all, as a lot of unique offers can only be completed once, and after that there's no way of proving what occurred. Dropping a company an email to tell them you've fulfilled your role is one thing, but providing them with videos, pictures, testimonials or other feedback is a much more effective strategy.

Whatever you choose to do, just ensure someone else is there documenting the fulfilment. If need be, invite the company representative down, so they can be a part of your offer. If you've received an expensive product for free, this is a nice courtesy, and is one of the strongest ways to build a bond for the future.

Another option is to invite the local paper to watch you complete the offer, and then they'll take care of all the documentation. This is a bit pointless if you've only received a free bag of crisps, but if your unique offer has a humorous or fun element, this always goes down well. It'll be even better received by the person who sent you the product if they're a PR rep, as in effect you've given them free publicity.

5 – How will you gather attention for the offer?

Although not particularly necessary, it can be nice to try and promote what you are doing before and after it has occurred. It'll help get your name out there, and is another way for the company to see you are working hard for your free product.

All of the online tools are great for this as they are designed for sharing. Blogs, videos and photos can be shared among friends, so you should at the very least make all your friends aware of what you are doing, and try to get them involved. If you're using the job unique offer, consider running a press release. The charity unique offers lend themselves well to gaining attention from local groups and papers.

Another good strategy is setting your unique offer in a public place. You'll need to check with your local council before doing this, but if you can get the go-ahead from them, a public demonstration completing your offer is a good way to build up hype and support for you.

These five steps complete your role in fulfilling the offer, and you can put as much time and effort into them as you feel is fair for the cost of the product you've received. If we apply bartering principles, you should try to offer equal value in return for the product. All of the above suggestions are free, so it's really just a question of time.

Not every product you get for free needs a huge fanfare, massive hype and many man-hours of planning, so apply logic in terms of the size of the company as well. If you get a product from a small company, it's unlikely they'll send you anything again, so there's less need to wow them. By comparison, a PR agency with many clients and really nice employees is deserving of a good return for their freebie.

How to Feed Back

When everything is done, and you're happy you've fulfilled your role, it's time to contact the company and report back on how you've done. This is a trick I missed for months, and in return I missed out on limitless future goodwill. I would fulfil the offer, post the results online, and didn't even tell the company it was there. Madness!

At the time it was because I thought the companies sending me freebies wouldn't actually care about the completion of the offer. I (wrongly) assumed they would send the product, trust me to do what I said, and then move on to the next prospect for product coverage. This was justified in my mind, as nine times out of ten I wouldn't get a follow-up response from the company, therefore reinforcing my view they didn't care.

But I was missing a major trick. By not feeding back to the companies, it meant the next time I contacted them it was almost like doing it from scratch. Only many months later would I take the time to remind them of what I had done, and show them the results. This was pointless for most marketing, sales and PR contacts, as by this point they had moved on to other projects and the feedback was of no use to them.

When you are sent a product it's because the company wants to see results in the short term. Never taking the time to follow up means the company doesn't get this chance, in which case you may as well have not completed the offer; the company couldn't see the benefit from it when it mattered.

Remember, we want to wow companies, and we want to do it as soon as possible after the product arrives through our letterbox. They can then pass the data to their bosses, or see a clearer improvement in their business and attribute it to the work you have done.

We've discussed the means of documentation above, so the majority of the work you need in providing this feedback is already there and waiting. Gather together the documentation you have (whether it be press cuttings, video, photos, web links, reviews, or whatever) and put together a concise email that explains you completed the offer and includes the links. If all you've done is write a review then that's fine to include. Not every piece of feedback has to have the same attention to detail as a global product launch. The important thing is that you've done what you were asked and provided proof.

The email should close by thanking the company for their product and proposing a new unique offer should they want to send you anything in the future. You can go back to the drawing board for this one, and take a look at the other products the company has. You've already wowed them once, so this is the best possible time to push for another product.

Ask for a Testimonial

If you're dealing with a responsive contact then they might give you a well done or a nice bit of positive feedback. Once this is received you've got two choices:

A)   Ask if you can quote their feedback.
B)   Ask them to provide a testimonial.

Use the first option if you feel the email contains the perfect quote about you, and go for the second if you want them to comment on a different part of the offer. It's a bit cheeky, as at this point you've both completed your role in the bartering process, and this is an extra bonus. But hopefully they'll be so happy with the work you've done, it should come naturally.

The perfect time to ask for a testimonial is just after you've completed the offer, and if you wait even a few weeks it becomes harder to get positive feedback. So go for the feedback early on.

Unhappy Companies

Once you've completed the offer the company should be ecstatic. Annoyingly, there can be occasions where companies are not happy with the desired results. This is rare, but it's important you're taught how to handle this effectively and turn the situation in your favour.

The number one reason for client unhappiness is a misrepresentation of the product. Or, in other words, you've said something they don't like. This is inevitable if you've been sent a product that is rubbish, and you've read my comments at the start about not lying to companies, and not lying to the public. If you've promised to talk about a product, and it is rubbish, you can send it back or tell the truth.

This honesty won't always anger a company, so please don't be put off in that respect. Without reviews, marketing and PR agencies would have a far harder time exposing their products, and part of this means not everything said will be favourable.

So what I've always done is, no matter how bad the product may be, look for one positive aspect. This will always exist; otherwise a company simply would not put their product to market. An MP3 player with a terrible design may have great audio, or a book may have a terrible plot but a good ending. Either way, when you talk about a product, look from both sides.

Then, when talking about the product, I will emphasise the good and the bad, leaving people to make their own minds up. That way, if a company complains about the bad, you can pre-empt this with your comments about the good parts. There's no deceit as you've still been truthful, and people get a fairer opinion of a product.

The other way this can go is if your offer is poor in itself. So if you offered to mow the lawn of a company they may feel your workmanship wasn't good enough. This should be dealt with in the very same way as if you were contracted to do the same work for money.

If a company is unhappy they could complain and you are under no obligation to provide a refund (i.e. the product back). You may decide as a gesture of good will to return a product, or offer them something else in return (that doesn't cost you any money).

Whatever the case, if you get a negative comment, reply immediately stating that you will review this and get back to them tomorrow. Giving yourself a day to think of the best response allows them to calm down, and gives you a better chance to come up with an appropriate solution.

I'll reiterate that this is rare, and companies should already have a pretty good idea how well your offer will work out – otherwise they wouldn't have taken you up on it in the first place.

If all goes well it's time to think about getting product number two.

chapter 13

Refine and Improve

If your first freebie is going to be the hardest, then it makes sense that there needs to be a stage of refinement and improvement over time that will make things easier in the future.

As you gain confidence and start to see that the methods in this book work, you'll at the same time be working towards an improved offer that works consistently and gains company attention.

So first it's really a case of looking back at the steps you took that resulted in the product being sent, and a happy company at the end of the process. This goes all the way back to the creation of your persona, right up to the final congratulatory email, and each step can be reconsidered.

Refinement is also key when we consider that you really want to try and stand out from the crowd to get businesses to notice you. Remember how we talked about scaling this concept, and ensuring the principles are as effective in five months' time as they are today? Well, to give you the best chance of getting a product, the more you have honed these skills, the better you will be, and the stronger you will appear compared to other people. Success leads to more success, and developing your ability to get free stuff is a rewarding process that you can make your own mark on within a very short time.

Persona Refinement

With the persona, you'll need to look at which version you felt most comfortable with. Did companies seem to respond better when you had more confidence, or did it come across as cockiness? Were you enjoying being a certain persona over another one? Or did the concept of personas not really fit, and you were happier just being yourself?

Whatever the case, think back to the time when you felt you had the most charisma, and really got the attention of a company. This may be the first company who took your offer seriously, or a phone call that went really well. It'll be different for everyone, but you'll know when things were going well, and this is something you should try to capture for all future conversations.

Remember when we initially showed our persona to friends and family? You'll already have a rough idea what they preferred, so try and match this up to your own experiences. If people liked a particular aspect, then try to tweak this and make it better. People loved the hat you wore? Then try something similar. Friends didn't like the way you looked deeply in their eyes during conversations? Then change it.

The idea isn't to start everything from scratch, nor to assume you've perfected the process in one go. Little tweaks here and there can make a world of difference, and you may find just changing something makes you feel better, rather than having a drastic impact on the people whom you speak to.

Unique Offer Refinement

This works in two ways. The first is that you will be refining your offer for each company anyway, to better suit their needs and the products they sell. The other side of this is refining your unique offer to make it better for all the companies you contact.

Let's say your offer is something that gathers public attention. All the online options, journalist strategies and charity offers fit this mould. You can improve this offer by spreading awareness and telling other people about what you achieved with the first freebie. People love hearing about what others have received for free, and it's very easy to gather attention by talking about your achievements. If this is done online, or through newspapers, then you'll attract further attention as well.

You can improve the offer simply by trying to attempt something bigger and better next time. If you've chosen setting a world record for your unique offer, then the logical step is to try and beat it, with a different product. Or if you got on really well with the original company, you can contact them again and attempt a second go.

The more traditional bartering options, like the jobs offers, fit into this too. If you did a great job for someone in return for a product, then try to make this even better the next time around. Alternatively, try and make the process quicker, so you've got more time for requesting other free products.

Contact Refinement

Unless you managed to get something sent on your first try, it's likely you chose a few different contact methods along the way. Thus, you will have some idea of which ones worked and which gathered a poor or nonexistent response.

For me, face to face didn't work for a long time, and so I focused on phone and email. Your experiences may differ depending on your persona and personal traits. Once you find something that works, then stick to it. If you've made an email template that gathers a good response, that's the one to go for.

The added bonus is you can improve these methods of contact by adding some information on your last unique offer and how well it went. Testimonials act as great positive feedback to get other companies involved, so including these is win-win.

Here We Go Again

Once you've finished this process you'll be ready to start the whole thing again. This time will be quicker and more successful, and you can continue to refine over time as you get better and better.

chapter 14

30-Day Challenge

You now know everything there is to know about how to get companies to send you products for free. From personas to unique offers, we've covered it all. If you've made it this far and are ready for the challenge, but still unsure how to start, this chapter sets out a target plan that you can follow.

I still won't tell you exactly what your persona or offer should be, as only you can discover this, but I will set out a 30-day plan you can use to attempt the challenge for yourself.

I've tried to keep each day in the challenge to 30 minutes or less, so you can attempt this around your day-to-day life, but please don't feel like this is a continuous 30 days. If you only have 15 minutes a day then it's fine to cut down the time on tasks or spread them over a longer time. This isn't a strict regime, so if you miss a day simply pick it up and carry out those activities the next day.

The goal is to have fun, contact companies and get some freebies. Easy!

Day 1

- Browse the Internet to find types of products that you'd like (e.g. a book).
- Don't look for specific products or brands at this early stage.
- Find ten manufacturers of the product type.
- Write down their details in a spreadsheet.
- Rate each one of a scale of 1-10, so you can tell which you'd prefer.
- Add a comment for each one about their recent news/new product launches.

Day 2

- Look for contacts at each of the ten manufacturers.
- Try to find someone in PR, marketing or sales.
- PR agencies are the preferred choice.
- Write down contact details, and their name.
- Add a comment about each person, based on what you can find online.

Day 3

- Create a persona.
- Find someone who inspires you.
- Discover their secret.
- Add a personal touch.
- Try it on yourself.
- Try it on others.
- Improve the persona based on feedback.

Days 4-5

- Create a unique offer.
- Try to think what each company would want, that you could offer.
- Don't spend any money in doing this.
- Re-read the example offers, and see if you could change these to fit your skills.
- Consider your friends and how they could help.
- Discuss the offer with friends.
- Improve the offer based on feedback.

Days 6-7

- Decide on your preferred contact method.
- Draft a conversation in this format.
- Mention the offer, your skills, contact details, and why you chose the company.
- Contact the three companies with the lowest score on your chart.

Days 7-8

- Refine the unique offer/contact method.
- Look at any feedback you have received; if no feedback, leave this for another day.
- Take on board any negatives/reasons for refusal.
- Consider if the offer could be improved or changed.
- Make contact with the next three companies, based on their score.
- Ensure all communications are tailored to each company.
- Respond to any positive replies with further details.

Days 9-12

- Repeat the steps from days 7-8.
- Contact the remaining four companies with improved offers.
- Consider changing the persona if this doesn't seem to be well received.

Days 13-15

- Make a second contact with any companies yet to reply.
- If no replies, start preparing a list of 10 more companies.
- Fulfil the offer for any products received.
- Notify the company you will be completing the offer.

Days 16-20

- If no replies and no products, make contact with the next 10 companies.
- If the offer has been fulfilled, try to spread awareness.
- Contact newspapers or spread the word online.
- Contact the company to tell them the offer has been completed.
- Provide proof of completion.
- Ask for feedback.

Days 21-25

- If no replies and no products, make second contact with companies.
- Ignore those contacted in the first wave.
- If product arrived, repeat steps from days 8-10.
- If offer fulfilled, then refine offer.
- Notify original companies who didn't send you a product of what you did for their competitor – try to encourage them to send you products.

Days 26-30

- By now you should have received a product.
- If not, consider a different product category/persona/offer.
- Or try using friends more in future attempts.
- Try to chase companies contacted for final answers.
- Ask those who said no to explain why in more detail.
- Contact those who said no with alternate offers.
- Alternatively, repeat steps on day 10 if product received.
- Start refining your offer for future development.
- Review what did/didn't work.

chapter 15

Ready, Set, Go!

I'm confident that following the steps in the book will result in free products. I hope the above process helps explain the concepts in detail, and gives you the confidence to give this a try.

Not everyone will come up with a perfect offer in one go and that can be discouraging, but this really is worth the time and energy when it all goes right. To break the cycle of vouchers and coupons and instead get free full versions of products is a powerful thing, and it's not something everyone knows how to do.

Armed with the knowledge in this book, you now know something unique. What's more, you'll have a plan of attack based on your own strengths in personality and conversations. I hope you've discovered some new talents you may not have known you had, or been sent some fantastic products that you never would have seen.

All that remains is to wish you the best of luck in your journey. If you get stuck or need advice, I can be contacted by email at mike@blagman.co.uk and will do my very best to point you in the right direction.

Good luck! *Mike Essex*